Cub
Scout
Games

The Scout Association,
25 Buckingham Palace Road
London SW1W 0PY

Cub
Scout
Games

Compiled by:
Joyce Trimby.

Editors:
Valerie Peters
Joyce Trimby.

General Editor:
Ron Jeffries.

Illustration:
Bob Dewar.

Design:
David Goodman.

First Edition
First Printing
May 1972

Printed in Great Britain by
Richard Clay (The Chaucer Press) Ltd.,
Bungay, Suffolk

Contents

Foreword

The games in this book have been contributed by many Leaders who, at the request of Headquarters, sent in well-tried and favourite games played with their Packs. Naturally many were duplicated, many are already well-known, but it is hoped that among them there will still be those which will be new even to the 'Old Hands', and others will be reminders of good games half forgotten.

To the many new Scouters who will use this book, a word of advice. To be successful, games must be played to suit your Pack, your environment, the number of boys and their temperament. Study the game and adapt it to suit your circumstances. No rules are sacrosanct.

It is often helpful to try out a new game with a few boys. Your Sixers and Seconds will be happy to experiment with you, whereas an experiment with the whole Pack may result in chaos and a potentially good game is lost to the Pack for ever.

Some games may appeal more to the younger Cub Scouts and can be used more profitably when the older boys are off on some activity with another Leader.

A wide variety of games is included and good programme planning will result in a balance between the energetic and noisy game—noise at the right time is a necessary outlet for Cub Scouts; the game which trains the senses and the mind; the technical training game bringing in the Arrow Tests; and all the others grouped under headings which we hope will be an aid to programme planning. The guiding principle should be 'Decide upon the purpose of your game'. The purpose may well be just for fun, but a definite purpose there should be.

A separate section has not been included for the Extension (Handicapped) Cub Scout. Many of these games can be adapted to suit a particular handicap and then the adaptation should apply to the whole Pack—'This is the way we play this game in our Pack'. Our policy is to integrate a handicapped boy into a Pack whenever possible. Although such a boy will usually make tremendous efforts to keep up with the Pack there will be games which are unsuitable for him. The rest of the Pack need to play the boisterous games which would be impossible for the physically handicapped Cub and these should not be denied them. An opportunity should be made for the boy to participate—to act as scorer, or a base man to renew 'lives', etc. There are a few pages at the end of the book where you may note games from other sources but no doubt these will soon be filled and a valuable supplement to this book will be your own Games Book.

It should be noted that throughout the book the term 'leader' applies to the leader of that game and not the leader of the Pack.

We hope these games will provide many enjoyable hours with your Pack, and we should also like to think that we shall share this book with those not in Scouting— with other Youth Leaders, Teachers and all those who find delight in the happiness of young people.

Activity Games

These games are suitable for the beginning of the Pack Meeting, and many can be played while the Cub Scouts are still arriving. They need little equipment and may be played in or out of doors. The games are intended to satisfy the Cubs' need for strenuous physical activity and are all free in movement and should result in physical relaxation leading on naturally to periods of mental activity.

Round the World

Equipment: Set of cards—roughly 8; felt-tipped pen.
Preparation: Write on each card the names of various countries and distribute these round the room.

The Cubs are all travelling by air round the world. When the leader calls out the place to visit *en route*, the Cubs all fly to the country in which the place is situated, e.g. the White House—the Cubs run to the U.S.A.

The Elephant Hunt

Equipment: Football; chalk.
Preparation: 2 chalk lines are drawn about 3 metres (3 yds.) apart in the centre of the room.

This is elephant country. All the leaders are hunters and the Cubs are elephants. The hunters are ranged either side of the lines and must not enter elephant country. The hunters catch the elephants by hitting them below the knees, with the football. Any Cubs who are caught become hunters until there is only one elephant left as the winner.

Submarine Dive

Equipment: Piece of chalk.
Preparation: Draw a number of small chalk circles—submarines—around the room with one less than the number of Cubs in the Pack.

The Cubs hop, walk or run round the room according to the direction given by the leader. When he calls 'Submarine dive !' each Cub tries to get into a submarine. The one Cub who is left out stays on a submarine for the next game and so gradually the submarines become occupied. The winner is the one who gains the last vacant submarine.

Activity

Rabbit down a Hole

The Cubs stand in pairs facing each other and holding hands to make arches. The pairs are spaced at random around the room.

The Cubs are respectively 'rabbit' and 'hunter'. The 'hunter' gives chase to the 'rabbit' who dodges around the trees, finally going down a hole, i.e. running into an arch and standing with his back to one of the Cubs making the arch. This Cub immediately breaks away and becomes a 'rabbit' and the ex-'rabbit' becomes part of the arch. If the 'hunter' catches the 'rabbit', they change roles.

Whale Ahoy!

Equipment: A paper or sock ball, or beanbag.

One boy is selected to be the 'whale', he may run freely about the room. The rest of the Cubs each choose a position and since they are 'rocks in the sea' they may not move. The aim is to 'harpoon' the 'whale' by hitting him with a ball. Whoever hits him takes his place as the next 'whale'.

The skill of the game lies in passing the 'harpoon' from 'rock' to 'rock' in an endeavour to corner the 'whale', rather than the Cubs taking random shots. This is good training in playing for the game rather than for the individual.

Shops

Equipment: Piece of chalk.
Preparation: The names of various shops are written on the floor around the room, e.g. greengrocer, butcher, chemist, fishmonger, newsagent, etc.

The leader tells a story mentioning items for sale in the various shops. When an item is mentioned the Cubs run and form a queue at the correct shop. Anyone who goes to the wrong shop, anyone pushing and the last Cub in the queue, loses a life.

Note: This game is best played with a Pack of 24 or less.

Tail Tally

Equipment: 1 rope per Cub; a whistle.

One Cub from each Six is a 'catcher'. All the other Cubs have a 'tail', a length of rope which they tuck in their jerseys. The 'catchers' try to snatch as many tails as possible in a given time. A Cub who loses his tail goes to a 'pen' from which he may be released if the 'catcher' from his Six gives him a tail.

When the leader blows the whistle, the Sixes return to their corners and count their tails, including those that their 'catcher' has snatched.

Fishes in the Sea

Equipment: 1 rope per Cub; 1 whistle.

The Sixes line up in files. Each Cub has a 'tail' attached by tucking a rope under his jersey. Each Six is given a name of a different fish.

When the leader calls 'The sea is rough and washes out all ——' (he mentions one of the 'fishes') that Six has to run round the room where Assistants are standing as 'waves'. They will try to catch the 'fish' by pulling out their 'tails'. After a count of ten, any Cubs not caught make a file again. Any who are caught stay in the sea, become 'waves' and help to catch. Each 'fish' is mentioned in turn and if the call comes 'The sea is very rough and washes out all the "fishes"', all the Cubs have to run away.

Block Busters

Equipment: 2 wood blocks; large ball; chalk.
Preparation: Draw 1 circle at either end of the hall, at least 2 metres (2 yds.) in diameter. Place the wooden blocks in the centre of each— these are the goals.

The Pack divides into two teams, one with their scarves on and the other team with them off, for identification. Each team is given their goal.

The object of the game is to knock over the block of the opposing team. The ball may only be moved by hand and may not be held. The Cubs may move anywhere as attackers or defenders, but may not enter a circle.

Activity

Desert Warfare

The commands are :

'Arabs !'—Cubs rush to one end of the room making war-like noises.

'To the Fort !'—Cubs rush to the other end of the room.

'Water Hole !'—Cubs kneel and scoop up water with their hands.

'Sand Storm !'—The Cubs crouch down and pull imaginary blankets over their heads.

'Camels !'—Two Cubs make a camel and a little one jumps on his back.

Note: 'Camels' is only called once and makes a glorious riotous finale.

Fill the Basket

Equipment: A pail or a large basket; as many balls as possible.

The leader has the basket and endeavours to keep it empty, throwing the balls as far away as possible. The Cubs do their best to fill the basket. See who wins at the end of five minutes !

Note: Paper balls can be made from newspaper covered with a thin paste and then tightly screwed up.

Nets

Two Cubs form a 'net', while the rest of the Pack are 'fishes'. The 'nets' try to catch a 'fish' by dropping their arms, with their hands held together, over a 'fish's' head. Once a 'fish' is caught it becomes part of the 'net' and when a fourth 'fish' is caught, the 'net' separates and becomes two separate 'nets'. The game goes on until the last 'fish' is 'netted'.

A variation on this game is:

Sheepdog Trials

Two Cubs link hands and are called the 'sheepdogs'. They chase the rest of the Pack who are the 'sheep' and if they capture one he is taken to the leader. When a second 'sheep' is captured he joins the first to make a second 'sheepdog'. This is repeated until all the 'sheep' are captured.

The Mystery Number

Equipment: A whistle.

The Pack forms a circle with the Sixers in the middle. The Sixers choose a mystery number known only to themselves. The Cubs march round in a circle chanting the number of each step they take. When they reach the secret number, the Sixers chase them. After ten seconds, the leader blows the whistle and the chase ends. Any Cubs who have been caught go into the centre and help the Sixers. The next number is decided upon and the game goes on until time is up and the Cubs who remain free are acclaimed as winners.

Note: As the chasers become more numerous, they must hold hands until the mystery number is reached. Set a limit to the mystery number. Anything over ten becomes tedious.

Dutch Football

Equipment: Piece of chalk; 4 balls.

The room is divided into four sections with chalked lines.
The Pack is divided into four teams, one standing in each section with a ball. On the word 'Go !' all the Cubs must hop on one leg and endeavour to keep the balls out of their section by kicking them with the foot they are hopping on. On the call 'Pack' they must all stop dead where they are and any section that has no balls gets a point. The leader should be quick to notice where the balls are when 'Pack !' is called, as they may easily roll into another section. For this reason, sock balls are recommended instead of ordinary ones.

Activity

This is my House

Equipment: Chalk.
*Preparation: Draw a number of circles on the floor, just large enough
for a Cub to stand in and two less than the Cubs in the Pack. These
are houses.*

One of the two extra Cubs is a 'rich man' and the other a 'policeman'.
The 'rich man' goes around the country buying up houses without the
owner's permission. He runs up to a house and says 'This is my
house!', whereupon the owner runs to another house and says the
same thing, and so the game goes on.

Meanwhile the police are on to the trail of all these people who remove without telling them, and the 'policeman' runs around trying to
catch them changing houses. When he does catch an owner on the
move, they change roles.

I'm a Great Big Whale

Equipment: Wool to tie round arm.

The Sixers stand in the middle of the room. They are 'whales'. The rest
of the Pack with wool tied (visibly) on their arms, line up at either end
of the room. They are little 'fishes'.

The 'whales' then chant, in deep whale-like voices, 'I'm a Great Big
Whale at the bottom of the sea.'

The 'fishes' reply in high-pitched fish voices, 'And I'm a little fish
and you can't catch me!'

The 'fishes' then race to the far end of the room and the 'whales' try
to catch them by breaking the wool on their arms. Any who are
caught become 'whales' and help to catch the rest of the 'fishes'. The
game continues until one little 'fish' remains as the winner.

Clear the Deck

The four sides of the room are given names, i.e. 'Clear the deck!';
'Man the boat!'; 'Shore leave!'; 'In the galley!'

When the leader calls out any of those commands, the Cubs rush
to that side of the room.

There are extra orders as well: 'Boom coming over!'—lie flat on the
floor; 'Admiral coming!'—all stand to salute.

No one is ever out but the last Cub to obey the order loses a life and
rolls down a sock or rolls up a sleeve.

**Note: In the original version of the game the four sides of
the room are Port, Starboard, Bow and Stern, although this
is merely a matter of choice.**

Witch Doctors

The Pack stand in a circle. The leader names every fourth Cub a 'Witch Doctor'. The Cubs spread around the room and at the word 'Go !', from the leader, the 'Witch Doctors' chase the other Cubs, putting spells on them by touching them. When a Cub has been 'bewitched' he must freeze until the spell is removed by a free Cub touching him. A time limit is fixed and if all are not 'bewitched' in that time, the 'Witch Doctors' have lost.

Note: The 'Witch Doctors' should be distinguished in some way, e.g. by a scarf round their arms.

A variation on this is:

Doctor Who and the Daleks

Three 'Daleks' and three 'Doctor Who's' are a suitable number for a Pack of 24. The 'Doctor Who's' turn their caps back to front for identification and the 'Daleks' wear their scarves back to front. At the word 'Go !' from the leader, the 'Daleks' chase the rest of the Pack. If the 'Daleks' touch anyone, that Cub must freeze, until he is released by the touch of a 'Doctor Who'.

No one is out and no one ever really seems to be caught when the time is up, but it is a splendidly exhausting game !

The game should be played for roughly two minutes before the 'Doctor Who's' and the 'Daleks' are changed.

Jack Frost

A game to be played in the dark.

Equipment: Torch.

One Cub, 'Jack Frost', stands in the centre of the 'frozen lake'. The lights are put out and everyone runs around on the 'lake'. When the leader shines a torch, the sun is shining and everyone rushes to the edge of the 'lake' in case the 'ice' breaks. The Cubs try to touch the wall (which represents dry land) before they are caught by 'Jack Frost'. Those captured will help 'Jack Frost' next time.

Circle Games

These games are mostly energetic but manage to keep the Cubs in some sort of formation and thus circumvent their natural inclination to climb on chairs, tables or up the wall! These games are good for the inexperienced Assistant to run. They are the family type of game—all the Cubs playing together.

Ball Pass

Equipment: 1 ball.

The Pack form a circle and one Cub has the ball. He passes it to the neighbour on his left and immediately starts to run round the circle, his aim being, to be back in his place to receive the ball when it has been passed right round the circle.

Note: Choose a boy from a different Six for each attempt.

Rucsac Scramble

Equipment: A set of cards, 1 per Cub.
Preparation: Write an item of camp gear on each card.

The Pack sit in a circle and the leader gives each Cub a card. One Cub goes into the centre, he is the owner of the rucsac. The leader tells a story about a Cub who went to camp with a badly packed rucsac, e.g. the coach shakes up on the way to camp, and the toothbrush gets mixed up with the sweets. When the leader mentions toothbrush and sweets, the Cubs holding those cards try to change places while the centre Cub endeavours to catch one of them. If he succeeds, then the Cub who is caught takes his place in the centre and the leader continues with the story.

C.U.B.S.

Equipment: Beanbag.

The Cubs sit in a circle with the beanbag in the centre and the leader gives them a letter in the order C.U.B.S. all the way round the circle. The leader calls out one of the letters and all the Cubs with that letter run right round the circle and back through their places into the centre—where they try to snatch the beanbag. The Cub who gets the bag is the winner.

Crash

The Cubs move around in a circle and the leader calls 'Sit down in . . .' and mentions a number. All the Cubs try to get to groups of that number, and those who do not succeed lose a life and have to adjust their uniform accordingly. There are many variations to this game, here are two:

1. The leader tells a story and whenever he mentions a number, everyone sits down in those groups.
2. The leader calls out various things related to numbers, e.g. blind mice—days in a week—fingers on a hand.

The Tín Game

Equipment: 3 empty scouring powder tins or washing-up liquid containers; 3 tennis balls; chalk. Preparation: Chalk the 3 points of a triangle out in the centre of the room, about a metre (3 ft.) apart. Fill the tins with sand and seal them off, then place them on the chalk mark.

A Cub stands in the centre of the triangle, ready to defend. When the leader calls 'Go!' the other Cubs with the tennis balls endeavour to knock over the tins. The Cub defending sets the tins up again as soon as they have been knocked down.

The object of the game is to get all three tins down before the defending Cub has time to pick them up. The Cub who knocks down the third has the honour of defending in the next game.

Defending the Fort

Equipment: Football.

The Cubs divide into two teams, the attackers and the defenders. The defenders form a circle holding hands and facing outwards; they choose their captain who stands in the centre.

The attackers surround the fort and try to kick the football in. It may go through the legs of the defenders or over their heads; if it does the latter, the captain may catch it and throw it out again. But once the ball touches the ground inside the circle the fort is captured and the players change sides.

In the Pond

Equipment: Chalk.
Preparation: Draw a large chalk circle in the centre of the room.

The Cubs all stand round the circle just outside the chalk line. The leader stands in the centre, and gives the following commands:

'In the Pond!'—all the Cubs jump into the circle.
'On the Bank!'—all the Cubs jump out.

If an order is given when all the Cubs are already in or out of the Pond, it should be ignored. Incorrect orders such as 'On the Pond' or 'In the Bank' should also be ignored.

Those Cubs who make two mistakes are out and the last remaining pair is the winner.

Up River

The Cubs stand in two's in a circle, one behind the other and both facing inwards, so that two circles are formed. The Cubs in the inner circle are the rocks in the river.

When the leader gives the order 'Up River' the outer circle Cubs start to walk around the inner circle. The next command given by the leader is 'Down River', at this the Cubs about turn and start walking in the opposite direction.

After this there are a series of other commands:

'Swift river'—the Cubs *run* in the same direction.
'Shoot the rapids'—they run in and out of the rocks.
'Indians'—the rocks make a noise like Indians.
'Under the bank'—this is for cover, they run on in the same direction until they reach their partner and squat down in front of him.

The last Cub home after the final command has been given surrenders a life and has to adjust his uniform accordingly.

Unmusical Bumps

Equipment: 1 whistle; 3 beans per Cub.

The Cubs march round in a circle. When the leader blows the whistle, they all sit on the floor. The last Cub to sit down surrenders a bean. Marching can be varied by hopping, skipping, etc. One variation to this game is when the leader tells the Pack a story and at a pre-arranged word all the Cubs sit down.

Circle

Hot Potato

Equipment: Beanbag.

The Pack sit in a ring with one Cub in the centre. The Cubs pass the beanbag at random across the circle which the centre Cub has to catch. When he does, he can have a seat in the circle, and the last one to handle the beanbag has to go into the centre.

Earth, Water, Air and Fire

Equipment: Beanbag.

The Pack sit in a circle with one Cub in the centre holding the bean-bag. He throws the bag at someone and shouts 'Earth!', 'Water!', 'Air!' or 'Fire!'

If it is 'Earth!', the chosen Cub must reply with the name of an animal, before the centre Cub counts to ten. If it is 'Water!', he must think of a fish, if 'Air!'—a bird and if 'Fire!'—whistle for the Fire engine.

Note: Once a creature has been named it may not be called again. If the Cub cannot reply in time, he changes places with the thrower.

Another variation of this game is:

Land, Sea or Air

The Pack sit in a circle with a Cub in the centre who is IT. If IT stands in front of a Cub and makes a rolling motion with his hands, the Cubs must give the name of an animal that lives upon land, before IT has counted ten.

Should IT pass his hands backwards and forwards over each other, palms down, to indicate waves, the Cub must give the name of a fish or sea creature.

If IT places his hands at either side of his head, and makes a flapping motion, the Cub must give the name of some bird.

Note: No player must give the name of any creature already given by a previous player.

Come Along

All the Cubs stand in a circle with their right arms outstretched with one Cub outside. He runs round the outside of the circle and grabs an arm of one of the other Cubs who follow him round. They go on collecting others, until there are about six to eight running round. Then the first runner calls out 'Home', and they all dash to get in the circle. The Cub who is left out is the new runner.

Express Post

Equipment: 1 beanbag; 2 boxes or chairs.
Preparation: List the names of some towns, one for each Cub in the Pack.

The Pack stand in a circle, the leader gives each Cub the name of a town. The beanbag is placed in the centre and the two boxes or chairs are positioned outside the circle as pillar boxes.

One Cub is the 'postman', who calls, 'I have a letter to deliver.' The players call out, 'Where from?' The 'postman' calls out the name of a town and runs away with the beanbag pursued by the Cub who represents that town. The 'postman' suddenly places the beanbag in one of the pillar boxes and makes a dash for the place vacated by the pursuing Cub. That Cub picks up the beanbag and tries to touch the 'postman' before he can get in. If he succeeds the 'postman' is sacked and the other player takes his place.

How do you like your Neighbour?

The Pack sit in a circle on chairs. One Cub is IT. His chair is removed and he stands in the centre. IT asks one of the players, 'How do you like your Neighbour?'

The Cub then replies, 'I don't like him.'

IT then asks, 'Who would you prefer?'

The Cub replies with the names of two Cubs in the circle. The two Cubs named may then change places, IT endeavouring to capture one of their seats. Alternatively, the Cub addressed may answer, 'I like him—but I am going to move!' This is the signal for everyone to change places. If IT obtains possession of a chair, the Cub left out becomes IT.

Space Race

Equipment: 2 balls of different colours for 'Spacecraft'.

The Cubs form a circle and are numbered 1, 2, 1, 2, round the circle. The odd numbers wear caps and the even numbers discard them. Two 'spacecraft' start from opposite sides of the circle, one held by the 'Odds' and the other by the 'Evens'. At blast off the 'spacecraft' orbit around the circle odds to odds and evens to evens. The object being for one 'spacecraft' to overhaul and pass the other.

House to Let

Each Cub brings a chair to form a circle and sits down on it. One Cub gets up leaving his chair empty and comes into the centre of the circle. This Cub has just moved into the district and is wanting a house, so he goes to sit on the empty chair. As he does so, the Cub sitting on the right of the chair moves into it and the rest of the circle start to move up, as the centre Cub tries to find a vacant chair. When he eventually does, the Cub who has vacated it (not the one who fails to move up in time) becomes the 'house hunter'. This keeps the game moving at a good speed.

Catch the Stick

Equipment: A broomstick.

The Pack form a circle, facing inwards. One Cub stands in the centre, keeping the broomstick upright by resting the palm of his hand on the top of it.

The leader gives a number to each of the Cubs, the centre Cub calls out one of the numbers and immediately removes his hand supporting the broomstick. The Cub with that number must try and catch the stick as it falls, if he succeeds he goes into the centre and the other Cub takes over his number in the circle. If he fails, the Cub in the centre tries another number.

Note: The stick should be merely balanced and not held.

A variation on this game is:

Parachute Drops

Equipment: A supply of balloons.

The Cubs stand in a circle and the leader gives each a number, in sequence round the circle. One Cub with a balloon stands on a chair in the centre. As he drops the balloon he calls a number and the Cub with that number tries to catch the balloon before it reaches the ground. If he succeeds the Cub picks up the balloon and stands on the chair, and the first parachutist returns to the circle and takes his number.

Clap and Catch

Equipment: Football.

The Pack forms a circle and the leader stands in the centre with the ball. He throws it to each Cub at random who has to clap before he catches it. If a Cub fails to clap or claps when the ball is not being thrown to him he loses a point and has to stand on one leg. When he loses another point he must kneel, and finally, if he loses a third point, he is out and has to sit down.

Note: This is a good game to fill in an odd moment. It is not really necessary to have points—just good fun.

Head It! Catch It!

Equipment: Football.

The Pack form a circle and the leader stands in the centre with the football. He throws it to a Cub calling 'Heading!' or 'Catching!' and the Cub responds accordingly and if he fails, sits down.

The leader then complicates the game by shouting the same commands but expecting the Cubs to respond with the opposite action.

Steptoe and Son

Equipment: Rag ball.

The Pack form a circle and two boys go into the centre. They are 'Steptoe and Son' (or any other pair of characters who are currently in vogue). 'Steptoe' guards his 'Son' as the Cubs in the circle try to hit him with the ball. The Cub who is successful in hitting the 'Son' comes into the middle to be 'Steptoe' and chooses his own 'Son'.

Note: The skill lies in passing the ball quickly, so that the two in the middle are kept constantly on the move.

Mopping Him Up

Equipment: 1 dish mop; a pail or bucket.

The Cubs stand in a large circle with the pail in the middle. They all hold out their hands. One Cub with the mop walks round the inside of the circle and taps someone on his hands. He then rushes to the pail, drops the mop in and tries to run back and take the other Cub's place. Meanwhile, the moment the Cub in the circle is tapped, he dashes to the centre, picks up the mop and tries to touch the first Cub before he has taken his place.

If he does not succeed he becomes the Cub in the centre.

Note: If the room is very long and narrow, the Cubs may be lined up at one end of it with the bucket at the other.

Six Relay Games

Here we have the competitive element in Cub Scouting. Cubs enjoy Six relays and will compete fiercely for their Six. At Cub age, the urge to compete and win is very strong, even primitive! To say they will play by fair means or foul would perhaps be too strong, but unless under firm control, foul means soon creep in! The problem is not often conscious cheating, but the will to win can cause infringements of the rules if this is not checked.

Self-discipline is in the early stages with boys of this age and relay games help to develop this. There are several ways in which the leader can help.

(a) A disciplined start and finish to all relays is essential—the Sixes in straight lines for the start and alert at the finish.

(b) A trial run or demonstration by Sixers means that all know what to do, thus avoiding arguments and ill-feeling.

(c) The development of a good Pack spirit, when the winners are cheered and the losers take defeat cheerfully, is fundamental.

Stock-car Racing

The Sixes line up in files. Each Cub is given the name of a car and when that car is called, he travels to the end of the room and back in the manner described, e.g.:

1. Rolls-Royce: this never goes wrong—the Cub runs.
2. Austin: has a flat tyre—the Cub hops.
3. Morris: is stuck in reverse gear—the Cub runs backwards.
4. Ford: very old model, can only go slowly—the Cub walks.
5. Mini: only small—the Cub runs, crouched down.
6. Humber: pulls caravan—the Cub tows his Sixer behind him.
7. Stock-car: everyone runs.

Kangaroo Hop

Equipment: 1 tennis ball per Six.

The Sixes line up in files, a chair in front of each. The first Cub grips the ball between his feet and hops round the chair and back to his place. He hands over the ball to the next Cub, who does the same. The first Six to finish is the winner.

Radar

The Sixes line up in files with their Sixers about 10 metres (10 yds.) ahead of them. The first Cub in each Six is blindfolded. The Sixers then change places and proceed to call the blindfolded Cubs by their Six name, that is, bringing them in by radar. The first Cub—'aeroplane'—to 'fly' home scores four points, the second three points and so on. The next Cub is blindfolded, the Sixers change again and the game proceeds until all the 'aeroplanes' are safely home.

Six Relay

Baking a Cake

The Sixes sit cross-legged in files, each Cub is given the name of an ingredient to make a cake, e.g. number 1—flour, number 2—eggs.

The leader describes the making of a cake.

When an ingredient is mentioned, the appropriate Cubs hop round to the end of the room and back. The winning Six must all be sitting in a line, cross-legged, at the finish of the game.

A variation on this game is:

Colour Relay Race

The Cubs line up in files and are given a colour, e.g. number 1 in each Six is green, number 2 is yellow, etc. The leader calls out an article with a specific colour. The Cubs of that colour run to the end of the room and back, e.g. Buttercup—number 2 runs.

Yet another variation is:

Shop Relay Race

Each Cub is given a shop. The leader calls out an article and the Cub with the name of the appropriate shop runs.

Cotton Reel Towers

Equipment: 7 cotton reels per Six.

The Sixes line up in reverse order—the youngest in front. There are 7 cotton reels in a pile in front of each Six. The first Cub runs up and puts one reel on top of another, the second Cub puts one on top of that and so on until a tower is built.

If a Cub knocks the tower down, he must rebuild it—but his Sixer may come out and help him.

Mixture

Equipment: Chalk.
Preparation: Chalk 2 lines across the room some distance apart.

The Sixes line up in file order behind the first line. When the leader calls 'Go!' number 1 in each Six has to cross over the other line in any manner he wishes, e.g. hopping, running, etc.

As soon as he reaches the second line, number 2 in each Six starts going forward in any manner he likes, although different from number 1. The game goes on until all are over. The winning Six is the one who is first sitting cross-legged in file.

Threading the Needle

The Cubs join hands in their Sixes and hold up their arms like arches. The leader holds up his fingers to indicate a number. If he holds up— for example—3 fingers, this means that the Sixer is to lead the way through the third arch. The Cubs must keep hold of hands and follow their Sixer.

Journey to the Moon

Equipment: A national flag for each Six.

The Cubs sit in a circle in their Sixes and number off within their Six.

The flags are placed in the centre. The leader calls a number and the 'orbits' (the maximum is three 'orbits'). The Cubs with that number collect their flags from the centre, run out of the circle through their own space, 'orbit' the number of times called by the leader and dash back through their space to place their flag on the 'moon'.

Note: Flagstaffs are not a good idea as they would be dangerous in the final dash to the moon. The flags should be pasted on to strong card which will withstand some wear and tear.

Cattle Trains

Equipment: 1 chair per Six.

The chairs are placed in front of the Sixes at the end of the room. The Sixes stand in relay formation representing a 'cattle train'. The Sixer is the 'engine'. The other Cubs are in turn trucks of 'pigs', 'cows', 'donkeys', etc. At the word 'Go!' the 'engine' couples up with the first 'truck', races round the chair back to his Six, collects up the next and so on till the whole 'train' is on the move Each 'truck' load of 'animals' of course makes appropriate grunts, moos, etc.

As a variation, the leader can call for a certain 'truck', say, 'donkeys'. The 'engine' couples up with that 'truck' and races round the chair and back. This keeps everyone on the alert.

Six Relay

Whirling Wheels

Equipment: 1 beanbag per Six.

The Sixes line up as the spokes of a wheel, facing in a clockwise direction, with the Sixers in the centre.

The beanbags lie at the feet of each Sixer and when the leader gives the starting signal, they pick up the beanbag, run down the back of their Six and in a clockwise direction, round the wheel and back to the outside end of the Six. The beanbag is then passed up the Six to the Cub now at the centre. This continues until all the Cubs have had a turn.

The Whirling Heavens

The Cubs sit in a circle facing outwards. The leader names the Cubs in turn round the circle 'Cassiopoeia', 'The Plough', 'Orion', 'Gemini', 'Taurus'.

When the leader calls out one of the constellations, all those Cubs run round the outside of the circle and back to their places. The last Cub back has to turn inwards.

Flipping the Kipper

Equipment: For each Six: 1 cardboard flipper; 1 tissue paper fish; chalk.
Preparation: Chalk a large frying pan shape for each Six in the centre of the room, and another in front of the Six.

The Sixes stand in their corners. One by one the Cubs in each Six have to fan their kippers up to their frying pan in the centre. The next Cub has to fan it back down to the other frying pan.

Note: It is perhaps wise to have some spare flippers. The kippers should be in different colours so that each Six knows its own.

The Rat and Egg Relay

Equipment: For each Six: 1 length of rope; chalk.
Preparation: Line the Cubs in file at one end of the room. Draw a circle in front of each Six. Chalk a boundary line at the other end of the room.

Each Six places a ball in the circle. When the leader calls 'Go!' each Cub in turn, holding the ends of the rope in either hand, drags the ball up the hall, past the boundary line and back down the hall again to his circle.

Round the Moon

All the Sixes line up at the end of the room. Each Cub places his hands on the waist of the boy in front and so the Sixes form a 'rocket'.

One chair is placed at the far end of the room opposite each Six, these are the 'moons'. When the leader calls 'Go!' the Sixes run the length of the room, round their 'moon' and back into orbit. As they pass base, the 'rockets' drop a section each time and the Cubs sit down there one by one. Until finally the 'nose cone'—the Sixer—returns home. The first team to be sitting down is the winner.

Blunderfoot

Equipment: Chalk.
Preparation: Chalk a series of stepping-stones on the floor. Some marked with a cross are unsafe.

The Sixes line up in file order. When the leader calls 'Go!' the first Cub runs over the 'stones', but if he steps on a bad one, he has fallen into the water and must start again. As soon as he is over the stream, the next Cub starts. The first Six with all its Cubs across and sitting down in line is the winner.

Six Relay

Speedway

Equipment: 4 stout sticks about 1 metre (3 ft.) long; 4 old tin lids; chalk.
Preparation: Mark out the floor according to illustration:

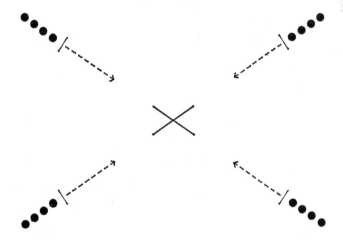

The Cubs line up in Sixes behind the line facing X in the middle of the floor. The first Cub in each Six holds the stick in the lid behind the line. At the word 'Go !' he pushes the lid along through X to the line opposite, turns and comes back, placing the lid on his own line. He hands the stick to number 2 and so on.

Note: The lid must be pushed through X and must clear the line on both sides.

Skiing Race

Equipment: For each Six: 2 shoe boxes; 2 garden canes; 4 washing-up liquid bottles; some sand.
Preparation: Weight the bottles with sand and place 4 out in front of each Six.

The Sixes line up in file order with the two shoe boxes and two garden canes in front of each. When the leader calls 'Go !' the first Cub in each Six puts a foot in each shoe box and with a cane in each hand slides ski fashion in and out of the obstacles in front of him, up to the far end of the room and back. This is repeated by each Cub, and the first team to finish is the winner.

Rocket Relay

The Sixes line up with a chair at the head of each, facing away from the Six. The chairs are 'launching pads' and the first Cub or 'rocket' stands on the chair awaiting the countdown.

When the leader reaches zero, the 'rocket' blasts off round the room, touching all four walls, and returns to the 'launching pad' where the next 'rocket' is waiting to be launched. The first 'rocket' lets off the second and returns to his Six.

Team Games

Cubs are only just emerging from the fiercely individualist and selfish stage—'Akela chose me,' 'Can I be next?' is a natural reaction.

Team games introduce them to the idea of striving for a group and not just for their own glory. These games develop good sportsmanship and require good umpiring from the leader. As with Relay Games, a trial run or demonstration is advisable to ensure that the rules are fully understood.

Team

Here I am!

Equipment: 1 large ball per team.

The Pack divides into teams of eight to ten Cubs. Each team forms a circle with one Cub with a ball in the centre. The Cubs number off round the circle and then the centre Cub goes out of the room.

While he is away, the Cubs change places so that the numbers do not run consecutively. The centre Cub returns and picks up his ball. When the leader calls 'Go!' the centre Cub calls 'Number 1' and he answers 'Here I am'. The centre Cub turns and throws the ball to him and he returns it. That number then sits down. The centre Cub continues through the numbers until all the team are sitting down. The first team seated being the winners.

Guards and Guerrillas

The Pack divides into two teams. One team stands in a line at the end of the room facing the wall. They are the 'Guards'. The second team, who are the 'Guerrillas', form a line at the opposite end of the room. They creep quietly up on the 'Guards'. When the leader of the 'Guerrillas' thinks that his team has crept as near as they dare, he gives the signal and all the team give one loud clap and then turn and run home. As soon as the 'Guards' hear the clap, they turn and chase the 'Guerrillas'. Any who are caught become 'Guards'. When there are no 'Guerrillas' left, the teams change roles.

Tunnels

Equipment: 2 footballs; 1 whistle.

The Pack divides into two teams and line up about 3 metres (3 yds.) apart facing each other. They stand, legs apart, with their feet touching those of their neighbours.

The leader throws a football down between the lines and each team tries to score a goal by sending the ball through the legs of the other team. The Cubs may only defend with their hands and must not move their feet. When the teams become adept at this, the leader can send in a second ball.

Nobody's Airship

Equipment: Length of rope or cord to stretch across the width of the room; supply of balloons.
Preparation: Hang the rope across the room about 1·5 metres (5 ft.) from the ground.

Team

The Pack divides into two teams standing on either side of the rope. The leader throws a balloon into the air above the rope. The object of the game, is for each team to make the balloon touch the ground on their opponent's side. The balloon must go *over* and not *under* the rope.

Tadpoles

Equipment: 1 ball; whistle.

This game is known by a variety of names, but here it is called 'Tadpoles' because the shape made by the teams is rather like a Tadpole.

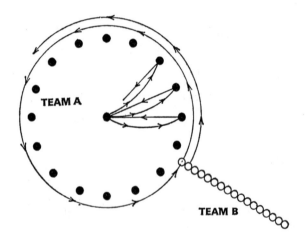

The Pack divides into two teams. Team A stands in a circle with one Cub in the centre, holding the ball. Team B stands in a line, like the tadpole's tail, coming from the circle.

When the leader calls 'Go!' the Cub in the centre of the circle starts to throw the ball to his team, one by one. Meanwhile, the Cubs in team B in turn run round the circle and back to their places. When the last Cub in team B is back in his place, the leader blows the whistle and team A stops. Team A says how many throws the Cub in the centre has made and when the teams change places, team B tries to beat team A's score.

Hopping Tommy

The Pack divides up into two teams and line up facing each other. The teams number off from opposite ends. When the leader calls a number, those Cubs, with their arms folded, hop towards each other and try to make their opponent lose his balance and put his foot down. The Cub who succeeds in doing this gains a point for his team.

Note: It is a good idea to make sure that the sizes of the opponents match. It is unfair to have a large boy against a small one.

Beating the Bounds

Equipment: 4 oil drums or metal pails; 2 large tent pegs or sticks.
Preparation: The 4 drums are placed at the four corners of a large square.

The Pack divides into two teams, each with a stick. When the leader calls 'Go !' the first Cub in each team runs round the square, banging each drum as he goes. If he misses a drum, he must go round again. When he finishes the circuit he runs to the back of his team and passes the stick to the front for the next Cub. The two teams make the circuit in opposite directions, one clockwise and the other anti-clockwise.

Chair Pass Ball

Equipment: Football; whistle.

The Cubs form two teams. A firm chair is placed at either end of the room as a goal for each team. A Cub from each team stands on a chair as goalkeeper. The ball may only be passed by hand. To score a goal, it must be thrown to the Cub on the chair and caught by him. There should be no running with the ball, or snatching from another player.

Note: The goalkeeper is changed after each goal.

Broomstick Hockey

Equipment: 2 broomsticks; 1 quoit.
Preparation: Place 2 chairs as goals at either end of the room. Put the quoit in the centre with the broomsticks on either side.

The Cubs form two teams and line up facing each other. They number off from opposite ends.

Team

The leader calls a number and the appropriate Cubs from each team run forward, pick up a broomstick and try to manoeuvre the quoit into their opponent's goal. If they succeed, they gain a point for their team.

Bombarding the Football

Equipment: 1 football; 20 tennis balls; chalk; whistle.
Preparation: Two parallel chalk lines are drawn, about 10 metres (10 yds.) apart, down the room. The centre of the area is marked by a small circle. Base lines are drawn about 5 metres (5 yds.) behind the other line.

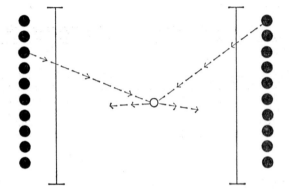

The Pack divide into two teams, each with 10 tennis balls. They stand behind the base lines. The football is placed on the centre circle. At the signal to start each team pelt the football with tennis balls, trying to make it roll over their opponents line and thus score a goal.

Balls from the opposing team may be retrieved and used again. Cubs must be firmly stopped from aiming when over the base line.

If a goal is scored, the balls are shared out again before the next game starts.

Snatch the Bobbin

Equipment: 3 cotton reels (bobbins); chalk.
Preparation: Draw a chalk circle at either end of the room. Place the 3 cotton reels in the centre of the room.

The Pack divide into two teams and line up at either side of the room. The teams number off from opposite ends. When the leader calls a number, those Cubs run from their places and pick up a bobbin from the centre to place in their goals. They then return to get the remaining bobbin. The Cub who is successful in getting this, and placing it in his goal, scores a point for his team.

Skittles
Equipment: 3 washing-up liquid bottles; 2 beanbags; 2 chairs.

The Cubs form up in two teams facing each other. The plastic bottles are placed in a row between them and at right angles to the teams. The chairs are placed between the teams and about 3 metres (3 yds.) from the bottles. A beanbag is put on each.

The teams number off from opposite ends. When the leader calls a number, those Cubs run to their team's chair, pick up the beanbag and standing on the chair try to knock the skittles down. They continue to retrieve their beanbag after each shot until one of them manages to knock over two out of three bottles. He gains a point for his team.

Warriors and Brigands

The Pack split into teams, one is the 'Brigands' and the other is the 'Warriors'. Each team has one end of the room as its base. The teams then line up facing each other and the leader gives various commands, e.g. ' "Warriors" two paces forward,' or ' "Brigands" one step back.' This goes on with mounting suspense (although three or four times are usually enough) until the leader says, ' "Warriors" (or "Brigands") attack!' Then the team ordered to attack gives chase as the others rush to their base. Any prisoners taken by the pursuing team immediately transfer to that team.

Rock Hurling
A game played by Stone Age Cubs!
Equipment: 1 paper ball per Cub; 2 sacks or large paper bags.

The Pack divides into two teams, each Cub with his paper ball. The teams line up facing each other about 4 metres (4 yds.) apart. One Cub from each team stands behind the opposing team with a sack. He is the 'headman' and has to catch or pick up all the 'rocks' that his team will send over the heads of the opposing team, and put them in his sack (he may have an assistant 'headman' to help him if he desires). The Cubs may collect any they can as they come over and hurl them back. The game ends when all the 'rocks' have been 'sacked'. Count the number which each 'headman' has collected.

Team

Block Relay

Equipment: 2 blocks of wood; chalk; 2 broomsticks.
Preparation: Draw chalk circles at each end of the room and place 1 block of wood in each circle. Place the 2 broomsticks in the centre.

The Cubs divide into two teams, each team lining up behind the circles on either side of the room.

The teams number off from the same end and when the leader calls a number, those Cubs run to the centre, collect a broomstick and manoeuvre the block of wood on their side, from one circle to the other.

Spaceship

Equipment: 5 coloured cotton reels; chalk.
Preparation: Draw a chalk circle in the centre of the room. This is the 'yellow planet' of KUBULA and the 5 cotton reels in the circle are the hidden 'treasure' of the planet. Four other circles should be drawn at the points of a cross. These are the 'spaceships'.

The Pack divides into four teams and one team stands in a line behind each circle. These are the 'crews' of the 'spaceships', and they number off. When the leader calls a number, the Cub in each team with that number runs up to the circle in the centre and collects one piece of treasure to take back to his 'ship'. He then returns to the 'planet' to collect some more treasure. When he finds that there is no more left, he raids other 'spaceships'. The rest of the 'crew' of each 'spaceship' sit behind their 'ships' and they are not allowed to defend the treasure. The winning team must have three pieces of treasure in their 'ship'.

Underneath the Arches

The Pack divides into two teams and number off from the same end.
Each team join hands along their line. The leader calls out consecu-
tive numbers, e.g. 4 and 5. These Cubs hold up their hands to form
an arch between them. The rest of their team starting at the first and
last numbers run through the arch, still holding hands, until finally 4
and 5 turn under their own arms. The first team standing up straight
is the winner.

Quiet Games

The Pack Meeting needs to have some con-
trast and after a noisy game the Cubs are
quite happy to play something quieter,
usually demanding some mental effort. For
some Cubs who do not particularly enjoy
the more boisterous games they are a welcome change.

Quiet games demand self-discipline from
the Cubs and the leader should insist on
quiet so that the game can be played pro-
perly. They are good games to play just
before an Investiture or before any occasion
when they are required to be attentive.

The March Hare's Game

Equipment: Pencil and paper per Cub.

Each Cub is supplied with a piece of paper and a pencil. The leader gives each Six a letter of the alphabet. The Cubs then draw something of their own choice beginning with that letter. The leader collects the drawings and says to the Pack that he will tell them several stories in the following weeks—each story incorporating all the drawings from a Six.

What am I?

The Cubs sit in a circle. One Cub goes outside the room, while he is away the others decide what he should be when he comes back. If they decide on a policeman, for example, they call him back and he has to ask each Cub in turn what he is to buy for himself. One will say black boots, another a whistle, another a torch and so on. If the shopper goes right round the Pack without guessing what he is, he must go out again, and the Cubs will choose something else.

The Snowball Story

The Pack sit in a circle. The leader begins to tell the Pack a story of a dramatic nature which arouses the Cubs' imagination. At an exciting point he breaks off and the Cub on his left continues. When the leader cuts him off, the next Cub has to take up the tale, until all the Pack have had a go. It's amazing what a weird story it turns out to be !

That reminds me

The Pack sit in a circle. The leader begins by naming something, perhaps a 'cloud'. The Cub on his left must say what a cloud reminds him of, perhaps 'rain', the next follows on with a connection for 'rain', perhaps 'umbrellas'. This carries on round the circle and back to the leader. Then the Cubs must work backwards, each Cub trying to remember what was said. Which Cub has the best memory ?

Who is missing ?

The Cubs walk round in a circle. When the leader gives a signal they all cover their eyes with their caps or their hands. The leader touches one of the Cubs on the shoulder and he leaves the room as quickly and quietly as possible, while the others still walk with their eyes closed.

When the leader calls 'Stop !' the Cubs stop walking and uncover their eyes. The first one to give the name of the Cub who is missing, is the winner.

Note : The Cubs should not walk round for too long a time, as they will become dizzy. Watch out for any Cubs who are cheating by peeping through their fingers !

Traveller's Trunk

The Cubs sit in a circle. One Cub is the 'Traveller' and goes out of the room. The rest of the Pack choose an item to take on holiday, e.g. swimming trunks, spade, book.

The 'Traveller' comes back into the circle and says that he wants an item, beginning with a certain letter, to fill his trunk. If there are Cubs who have chosen an item beginning with that letter, they stand up. The 'Traveller' has to guess what each is. He has only one guess for each Cub and if he is wrong the Cub sits down. If he is right, then the Cub comes and stands with him. After the 'Traveller' has had his guesses, all return to the circle and a new 'Traveller' is chosen. The winner is the 'Traveller' who gets the most things for his trunk.

Note : the leader should go round the circle, before the 'Traveller' comes in, to see that no Cubs choose the same item.

Submarines

Equipment: A scarf.

Two chairs are set up about 3 metres (3 yds.) apart, this is the entrance to the 'harbour'. One boy is blindfolded and stands in the entrance to guard it. The rest of the Cubs are 'midget submarines', and try to get through the entrance without being caught by the guard. They have to do this quietly so that he does not hear them. The leader should control the number moving, otherwise there is a stampede and it is no longer a quiet game !

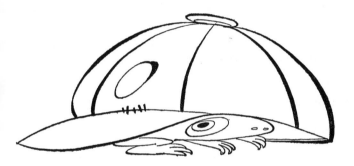

Where is it?

Equipment: 12 assorted articles; 12 Cub caps.

The Pack divides into two teams. They sit facing each other and between them are placed the twelve articles. When both teams have had a good look, each article is covered up with a cap. Then the first Cub in team A asks any Cub in team B where a certain article is. If the Cub uncovers the correct article, he may keep it for his team as a trophy. If he uncovers the wrong article, the point goes to team A and the article is covered up again. The first Cub in team B then asks the Cub in team A. When the last article is reached the team whose turn is next can claim the article if they know what it is. If they are wrong, it goes to the opposite team. If they are wrong, the guesses are passed backwards and forwards between the teams.

Note: If during the game, someone asks for an article that is already gone, it means a point for the opposite team.

The Musical Picture

Equipment: 1 sheet of drawing paper per Cub; 1 thick pencil or felt-tipped pen per Cub; record player; record.

The Pack sits in a circle, each Cub with his paper and pencil. The leader puts a record on the record player, and the Cubs begin to draw a picture. After about ten seconds the music stops and each Cub moves to the seat on his left. When the music starts again, he continues with the picture now in front of him until, once again, the music stops and he moves on to the next seat.

Note: A tape recorder would probably be better than a record player, unless the leader has a record which he does not mind being used in this way.

Steptag (from Australia)

This game is a variation on Blindman's Buff.

Equipment: 1 scarf.

The Cubs take up positions anywhere in the room. One Cub is blindfolded and he moves around the room, attempting to catch the others. Anyone who is in danger of being caught may move on, two or three steps in any direction. Once a player has moved three steps, he must stand still and hope for the best. The skill of the game lies in not using a step until necessary, because once the three steps are gone, the player must remain stationary. He can, however, crouch down or sway his body provided he does not move his feet.

We don't like Tea

The Pack sit in a circle with the leader. The leader asks one Cub, 'Do you like tea?', he must reply, 'No, I like . . .' and mentions something edible or drinkable which does not have the letter T, e.g. bananas, cocoa. So the game proceeds round the circle until a Cub makes a mistake or cannot think of anything. He then moves to sit on the right hand of the leader, which could be called the 'bottom' of the circle.

The leader then chooses another food, e.g. bread, and the Cubs must think of foods or drinks which do not include the letter B.

Note: The next round should always start where the previous one finished, otherwise some Cubs never get a turn.

Beavers' Bridge

Equipment: Torch; scarf; 1 stick per Cub.

This game is to be played in the dark.

The Pack divides into two groups of 'Beavers' and each group stands on a bank—either side of the room. The 'Beavers' want to build bridges in the stream—which is in the centre of the room. But they have an enemy, the 'Water Rat', who sits and watches them and plans to pull the bridges down.

One Cub is chosen as the 'Water Rat'. He is blindfolded with a scarf and sits on a chair at the top of the room with the torch. He shines the torch directly down the stream—this is the moonlight by which the 'Beavers' work.

Each Cub one by one creeps into the centre and puts his stick down. If the 'Water Rat' hears a noise, he shines his torch towards it. If he is successful in spotlighting the Cub, the leader calls the Cub out. Then the 'Water Rat' swings his torch back as the moonlight.

Quiet

Flagstaff Competition

Equipment: For each Six—4 canes; 6 rubber bands; some sticky tape; crayons or felt-tipped pens.

Each Six must design their own flag, join the canes together to make the highest possible flagstaff. They then erect it by fixing it to the back of a chair with the elastic bands and sticky tape.

The Mystery Sack

Equipment: Pencil and paper per Cub.

The Cubs sit in a circle in their Sixes, each Cub with his paper and pencil in front of him. The leader comes in with an imaginary sack. He puts it down, opens it and takes out an imaginary article which he describes by miming. Each Cub must then write down what he thinks it is.

Pirate Treasure

Equipment: Scarf; bunch of keys or anything else suitable for 'treasure'.

One Cub, the 'Pirate', is blindfolded and sits in the centre of the room with the 'treasure' in front of him. The other Cubs try to creep up from the sides of the room to steal the 'treasure'. If the 'Pirate' hears someone, he points in the direction of the sound. If he points at someone, then that Cub must return to his place.

The Growing Picture

Equipment: Pencil and paper per Cub.

The Pack sit in a circle, each Cub with his pencil and paper in front of him. The first Cub says what he wants to draw in his picture, e.g. a horse. So everyone draws a horse. Then the next Cub says what he wants, and so on, round the circle. The object of the game is for each Cub to try and make a picture out of these unrelated items.

This game will often find the artist. Most Cubs will produce a jumble of items, but sometimes real skill in composition and drawing will be discovered.

Squiggles

Equipment: Pencil and paper per Cub.

Each Cub is asked to copy a line or a shape on to his piece of paper.
He then adds as many lines as he wishes to turn it into a picture.

A variation of this, is to give each Cub a large letter or number
which he converts into a picture.

Whip the Whisker

This is a popular variation of Pirate's Treasure.

*Equipment: A face mask—this may easily be made (if bought, Guy
Fawkes masks are the easiest to obtain); 2 sheets of tissue paper.
Preparation: Block up the eyes of the masks. Cut the tissue paper into
quarter inch strips and fix to the chin of the mask as a beard.*

The Pack are seated in a circle with one Cub in the middle wearing
the mask. The Cubs creep up and try to whip a whisker from the
beard without being pointed at.

Quiet

A variation—the 'Pirate' has a water pistol and shoots when he suspects someone is approaching. If he shoots wildly he runs out of ammunition! Not perhaps a suitable game to play on a newly polished floor!

A.B.C. Ship

Equipment: 5 beans for each Cub.

The Pack sit in a circle with the leader. Starting with the Cub on the leader's left each Cub has to say in turn . . .

1. The name of a ship—Arcadia;
2. The name of the Captain—Alexander;
3. The surname of the Captain—Anderson;
4. Sailing from Port—Aberdeen;
5. Sailing to Port—Alexandria;
6. With a cargo of—Apples.

They follow on through the letters of the alphabet and Cubs who fail to respond lose a bean.

Note: This is a good game for the beginning of a parents' evening. The Cubs can join in the game as they arrive. An Assistant can run the game and the Leader is free to welcome parents.

Shuffled Letters

Equipment: 26 strips of paper.
Preparation: Write a letter of the alphabet on each slip of paper and jumble the slips up inside a hat.

The leader picks a letter out of the hat. He announces to the Pack, who are seated in a circle, what the letter is. Then he gives a clue to the word he is thinking of, which begins with that letter. The first Cub to guess a word is given the slip of paper. The one with the most slips at the end of the game is the winner.

How many Birds in my Nest?

Equipment: 10 stones per Cub.

The Pack sit in a circle, with their store of 10 stones hidden in their caps in front of them. The first player takes several stones and holding them in his closed fist he turns to his left-hand neighbours saying, 'How many birds in my nest?'
    The neighbour has to guess how many stones the player is holding. If he is right, the stones are his. If he is wrong, then he must give the player the difference, e.g. if he guesses 6 and the player holds 4

stones, then he must give the player 2 stones from his store. At the end of the game each Cub counts his stones and the one with the most is the winner.

Note: Groups of six Cubs are ideal for this and it is an excellent game to play while waiting for a bus or a train.

Spillikins

Equipment: Medicine bottle; 6 matches for each Cub.

The Pack sits in a circle with the medicine bottle in the centre. Each Cub takes it in turns to place the match on top of the bottle, or on the matches already there. If a Cub knocks any off while putting his on, he must take back all those knocked off. The first Cub to get rid of all his matches is the winner.

Note: If the safety matches are given to the Cubs separately from the box, there should be no risk of fire.

Sense Training Games

Sense Training was one of the fundamentals of the Founder's policy and its value remains true today. The games in this section train the Cubs' senses of hearing, touch, smell and observation—sense of taste is usually sufficiently well developed in Cubs.

Our senses were originally given to us for our protection and even in this sophisticated world we live in now, a quick response to a message through our senses can alert us to danger, and if the senses are keen, life is infinitely more interesting and enjoyable.

Dominoes
Sight

Equipment: 1 or 2 sets of real card dominoes depending on the size of the Pack.
Preparation: Keeping 1 domino for each Six, the rest are distributed around the room.

The leader then gives each Six one domino and they set off to find a domino matching at one end. The Six with the longest chain is the winner.

Find the Missing Picture
Sight

Equipment: Set of picture postcards, 2 or 3 per Cub.
Preparation: Cut each postcard in 4, the leader retaining 1 piece of each. Scatter the rest of the pieces around the room.

The leader gives each Cub a piece of card and they must find the other three pieces to make up the picture. The first Six to form an Art Gallery of six complete pictures is the winner.

Note: When a Cub completes a picture he may start a second one if the leader has any pieces left.

Bean Shapes
Sight

Equipment: 1 bag of beans or pebbles per Six.

The leader gives each Six a bag of beans which they empty in front of them on the floor. When the leader calls out the name of an animal or an article, the Cubs try and arrange the beans in the required shape. The first to achieve this gains a point.

Alfie and Georgie
Sight

Equipment: Chalk; 1 (quarto size) card; pencil.
Preparation: Draw a picture of a Cub on the card.

The leader shows the Pack the picture of a Cub who is called 'Alfie'. While the Cubs are out of the room—perhaps playing a ball game out of doors—the leader chalks an identical picture in the centre of the floor. He explains to the Pack, when they return, that 'Alfie' has an identical twin 'Georgie' who is hiding somewhere in the room. The Cubs must look for him and when they find him they must not show where he is, but go and sit quietly at the end of the room.

Sense Training

Note: This game is surprisingly successful as it takes quite a time for the Cubs to notice 'Georgie' is chalked on the floor. Never leave one Cub looking by himself, this can make him feel very miserable. When there are about three still hunting, finish the game by showing them 'Georgie' drawn on the floor. The Cubs who discover 'Georgie' early in the game are completely entertained by the mystification of the others still searching.

Uncle George   Sight

Equipment: Blackboard; chalk; piece of paper and pencil per Cub.

The leader tells the Pack about Uncle George and at the same time draws his portrait on the blackboard, e.g. he has only one hair left on the top of his head, he has a moustache, etc.

Then the leader turns the board round and the Cubs have to draw Uncle George from memory.

Note: No drawing is allowed while the leader is sketching Uncle George.

Match It!   Sight

A game to play during an expedition to the country.

Equipment: A number of leaves, flowers, twigs or other natural items from the area of the expedition.

The leader gives each Cub a specimen which he must watch. When he has matched it, he takes it to the leader and will get an extra point for telling him what it is.

Note: This game can be played successfully without knowledge of the names of specimens, though obviously those who do know the names should be awarded an extra point.

Kim's Game

Equipment: 12 articles on a tray—ordinary items such as string, ink, rubber, calendar; piece of paper and pencil per Cub.

The Cubs sit in a circle and the leader shows them the tray full of articles for a few minutes, before covering it over. The Cubs must write down the list of the articles from memory.

Here are some variations on this game:

Throwing Kim's Game

The leader throws some articles to his assistant and after all have been thrown, the Cubs must write down what they are.

Sticky Kim's Game

Equipment: 1 sheet of (quarto size) paper per Cub—plus 1 for the leader; plenty of gummed paper shapes, probably 1 small packet between 2 Cubs.
Preparation: Make a simple design on a sheet of paper with the shapes.

The leader shows her designs to the Cubs for a few minutes and then they must go back to their corners and produce the design from memory.

Note: A variation on this game is to use gummed stars on black paper making the design a pattern of one of the constellations.

Square Kim

Equipment: Pencil and paper per Cub; chalk; 9 objects which are simple to draw.

The leader chalks squares as for noughts and crosses on the floor and in each square places an object. The Cubs look at them for a moment before the leader covers them up. Then on their pieces of paper, the Cubs draw each article in its square.

Sense Training

Kim Pairs

Equipment: 12 objects on a tray; pencil and paper per Cub.

There are three versions of this game which can be taken in natural progression :

1. The Cubs sit in a circle and look at the objects on the tray. The leader then mentions an object which relates to something on the tray, e.g. the leader says 'letter' and there is a stamp on the tray. Then the Cubs must draw a stamp on their paper.

2. The same procedure is followed, but the tray is covered and the Cubs must draw the related object from memory.

3. The leader now mentions an abstract idea related to one of the objects, e.g. the leader says 'Open' and there is a key on the tray. So the Cubs must draw the key from memory.

Smelling Kim

Equipment: A collection of dried foodstuffs which have a distinctive smell, e.g. tea, coffee, sage, rosemary, etc., each in an identical container or in a small square of muslin tied with cotton; paper and pencil per Cub.

The Pack sit in a circle with the containers in the centre, the leader identifies the foodstuffs. He then numbers each container and passes them round the circle. The Cubs must identify the foodstuffs by their smell and write the correct names against the numbers on their sheet of paper.

Hearing Kim

Equipment: 12 small articles—non-breakable and simple to spell, e.g. matchbox full of matches, a rubber, a pencil; paper and pencil per Cub.

The Cubs sit in a circle with the articles in the centre. Each Cub looks carefully at them, then the leader asks them to turn and face outwards. The leader then drops each of the articles in turn and the Cubs write down what they are, judging them by the sound they make as they hit the floor.

Note: It is advisable for the leader to test the sounds beforehand to ensure that they can be distinguished.

What is in the bag?

Equipment: 1 bag per Six; collection of 12 items for each bag, e.g. cotton reel, pen, safety pin; paper and pencil per Six.

Each Six is given a bag of articles and they must feel each article inside the bag and write them down from memory.

Note: If each bag is different, then the game may be played several times with the Sixes swopping bags.

What did I eat?   Taste

This game is fun at a party

Equipment: A variety of tasty trifles, with an identical selection for each Six, sweets, tarts and savouries; pencil and paper per Cub; 1 blindfold for each Cub.

Each Six is blindfolded and sits in its corner. The leader gives each Six an identical collection of titbits. When the Cubs have eaten their selection, they remove their blindfolds and write down what they remember eating.

Note: The leader should have a list of all the food so that he can check the Cub's lists.

What Happened?

Equipment: Pencil and paper per Cub.

The Pack sit in a line facing the wall with their pencil and paper. They are detectives. The leader and his assistant are burglars, they stand some distance behind the detectives and make a series of sounds which suggest some sort of robbery, including breaking and entering, e.g. opening a safe, counting money, opening an envelope, etc.

The detectives must write down what they hear and afterwards come and report on the robbery.

Note: One of the assistants should make certain that all the detectives are facing the wall and are not turning around.

Electrical Shock   Touch

Equipment: 1 bell or whistle.

The Pack line up in two teams, each Cub puts his left hand back to reach the right hand of the boy behind him.

The Cub at the head of each team holds a bell or a whistle. The leader stands at the back of the teams between the two last Cubs. He presses the hands of the last two Cubs simultaneously. They press the hand of the Cub in front and so on up the line until the leading Cub has his hand pressed and rings the bell or blows his whistle. The first team to ring the bell is the winner.

Mending the Ship's Engine   Touch

Equipment: 1 bag per Six; a collection of 12 assorted items for each Six e.g. cork, a cotton reel.

The Sixes line up and number off. A bag of items is placed at the far end of the hall, in front of each Six.

The leader is the 'Chief Engineer' of the ship. The Sixes are squads of 'Engineers'. When the 'Chief Engineer' calls out, 'The engines have failed, I need a cork, Number 4!'—Number 4 Cub in each Six runs up to his bag, feels for the cork and takes it to the leader. The first Cub to produce the cork gains a point for his Six.

A variation on this game is:

Blind Man's Purse

Equipment: 1 bag per Six; a selection of coins for each Six.

The Pack lines up in Sixes and number off. The bags of coins are placed at the far end of the room opposite each Six.

When the leader calls out a number and a sum of money, those Cubs run up to their bag and feel for the necessary coins.

Matching Pairs
Touch

Equipment: An identical selection of articles for each Six that come apart in 2 sections—a biro and a cap, a match box, a tin with a lid—roughly 12 articles per Six; blindfold for each Cub.

The Cubs have a good look at the articles, then they are taken apart and mixed up. The Cubs are blindfolded and they must try to put the articles together again.

Note: It is important that the Cubs see the articles before they are blindfolded, otherwise they have no idea what they are trying to do.

Mystery Parcels
Touch

Equipment: 1 article per Cub; some newspaper and sticky tape; paper and pencil per Cub.
Preparation: Wrap each article in newspaper.

The leader gives each Cub a parcel and the Pack sit in a circle. The Cubs have a moment to feel their parcel, before the leader calls 'Change!' and the parcel moves on to the next Cub in the circle.

After the Cubs have felt about twelve parcels, the leader asks them to each write down what they have felt. Then the Cubs open their parcels, place the contents in front of them and check their lists.

What can you hear?

A game for an expedition to the country.

Equipment: Paper and pencil per Six.

The leader sends each Six to a different area and asks them to write down a list of all the sounds they hear.

Note: To make the Cubs really listen, ask for a minimum number of sounds so that they have a goal to aim for.

Sense Training

Tom Tom   Hearing

Equipment: A stick, a drum or tin.

The Pack sit in a circle and the leader gives one Cub the stick and the tin. He taps out a well-known tune on his drum and the first Cub to guess what it is will be the next player.

Shipwreck   Hearing

Equipment: Blindfolds for half the Pack; whistle.

One end of the room is the 'harbour' and the rest of the space is the 'sea', over which there is a heavy fog. Half the Pack space themselves over the sea and sit cross-legged on the floor, they are the 'rocks'. The leader blindfolds the rest of the Cubs and they stand opposite the harbour. These are the 'ships' out at sea, who have to steer themselves safely through the 'rocks' listening for the 'shushing' sound that the 'rocks' make as waves break over them.

When the leader blows the whistle, that is the signal of the foghorn and all the 'ships' must steer for the 'harbour'. If any of the 'ships' touch the 'rocks', they remove their blindfolds and sit on the floor with the 'rocks', as wrecks. The successful 'ships' reach the 'harbour' safely.

Rattling Tins   Hearing

Equipment: 12 or more identical tins, e.g. typewriter ribbon tins; half the number of small objects to put in the tins—e.g. a match, some rice, a rubber; different coloured crayon for each pair of tins.
Preparation: Separate the tins into pairs and into each pair put a different object. Mark each pair of tins on their bases with an identifying colour.

The Pack sit in the circle with the tins in the centre—mixed up. Two Cubs working together shake the tins to find a pair. They may carry on shaking until one decides that he has a pair. He then turns over the tins to check by the colour. If he is wrong, he has lost and the remaining Cub challenges someone else. If he is right, the other Cub retires, and the successful Cub challenges someone else.

Note: This is best played with a small number of Cubs or at a Sixers and Seconds Meeting.

A variation on this theme is to play the game like **Pelmanism (pairs)** with the Cubs remembering where the tins are on the floor as each tries to identify a pair. There will be many failures at first until the Cubs start memorising where the tins are.

Midget Submarines
Hearing

Equipment: Enough paper balls to equip the Six with about 4 for each Cub; 1 beanbag; chalk; enough blindfolds for one Six.
Preparation: Draw a number of chalk circles at one end of the room. These are 'oil tanks in a harbour', the entrance to which is marked by two chairs.

The leader blindfolds a Six and gives each Cub a supply of paper balls which are 'depth charges'. This Six space themselves out before the entrance to the 'harbour'. The rest of the Pack line up in Sixes. They are 'submarines' and take it in turns to approach the 'harbour' as quietly as possible, to place the beanbag, which is a 'bomb'—on one of the 'oil tanks'.

If the Six sitting on the floor hear anything, they throw their 'depth charges' in the direction of the noise. If they hit a part of the 'submarine', that Cub becomes inactive and remains sitting on the floor where he was hit.

Each Six has a turn to guard the 'harbour' and the one with the most hits is the winner.

Do this—Do that

The Pack stand in a circle with the leader in the centre. When the leader swings his arms or bends his knees and says 'Do this', all the Cubs follow. But if the leader makes some action and says 'Do that', the Cubs ignore him.

This game is run on the same principle as 'O'Grady says' and 'Simon says' which can easily precede the 'Do this' or 'Do that'. If 'O'Grady says' is omitted, and the order is just 'Do this' or 'Do that', it is ignored. Any Cub who is caught out must sit down and the last Cub left standing is the winner.

Shops

Equipment: Chalk; 6 beans per Cub.

The Sixers choose a shop that they will represent. They stand round the sides of the room and the leader chalks a doorstep in front of each of them. The shops are not labelled.

The rest of the Pack scatter round the room. The leader calls out the name of a shop and then a letter of the alphabet. The first Cub to put his foot on the correct doorstep and ask for an article obtainable from that shop, beginning with the correct letter, receives a bean. After a given time the Cubs count their beans and the one with the most is the winner.

Shapes

Equipment: For each Six: 1 set of small cards; 1 bag, plus one for the leader.
Preparation: Cut each card into two shapes so that there is an identical set of different shapes for each Six and for the leader.

The leader gives a bag of shapes to the Six keeping one for himself. He feels in the bag and brings out a shape, holding it up to the Pack. One Cub in each Six searches in his bag for the same shape and the first boy to hold up the correct one, gains a point for his Six.

Note: The shapes must be returned to the bag each time.

Neighbours

Equipment: Blindfolds for half the Pack; a whistle.

The Pack form a circle, sitting on chairs, the leader and his assistant blindfold every other Cub. Those not blindfolded then leave the circle and walk round it until the leader blows the whistle. They then go and sit down in the nearest empty chair and start either to sing or make the noise of an animal. When the leader blows the whistle again they stop and each blindfolded Cub, in turn, tries to guess the identity of the neighbour on his right. If he is wrong, the leader can ask the Cubs to sing or make their noises again. When all the Cubs have been identified they change places with the blindfolded Cubs.

Flarepath

Equipment: Blindfolds for half the Pack.

Each Cub chooses a partner, if there are any Cubs left out a group of three may be formed. One Cub in each pair is blindfolded—two Cubs in the case of three. They arrange between them a whistle signal by which they will recognise each other.

Those Cubs who are not blindfolded form two lines facing each other in the centre of the room, and when the leader calls 'Go!' all the blindfolded Cubs, armed with the torches, attempt to reach their partners whom they recognise by the prearranged whistle. When they eventually find their partners, they stand by them and switch on their torches to form a flarepath.

Arrow Test Games

These games are designed to help the Cubs with their Arrow Tests. Arrow work should be introduced wherever possible through some activity. Passive listening is a very dull way of learning. Small boys have short memories and the games can be used not only for learning but also as revision for a whole Pack. It is also possible to pass some tests while playing a game.

Jungle Knowledge

Water Truce
Cub Scout Badge

Equipment: Chalk; torch.
Preparation: Chalk two parallel lines on the floor some distance apart.

These are the banks of the stream which runs down the centre of the room. The leader stands at one end of the stream and an assistant at the other end with a torch.

Half the Pack stand on one bank and half on the other, the Cubs are all jungle animals and have come down to the stream to drink.

The leader says:

> 'The pools are shrunk, the streams are dry,
> and we be playmates, thou and I,
> Till yonder cloud—Good Hunting!—Loose
> The rain that breaks our Water Truce.'

As long as the torch is on the sun is shining brightly and the Cubs may drink safely.

When the torch is off, it is clouding over and the rains have come. Then the Cubs must run to their corners because the Truce is over. The leader tries to catch the Cubs while they are running, but if the torch comes on while a Cub is being caught, he may shout 'Water Truce!' and be released.

This game can become fast and furious as the torch is switched off and on.

Bagheera's Bones

Equipment: A number of cotton reels or match boxes—at least 2 per Cub.

The cotton reels represent old bones from animals that Bagheera has killed. They are scattered over the floor of the room. The Pack are being taught by Bagheera (the leader) to hunt. Remember this description of how Bagheera moved:

'He could move so gently that not a twig would crack under his foot. He could keep so still, no one could see him in the shadows of the jungle.' Starting at one end of the area, Bagheera moves slowly forward, the Pack behind him. Each Cub tries to pick up a bone without Bagheera seeing him. Bagheera looks round frequently and any Cub who is seen to move has to go right to the back of the Pack and start again. The Six who has collected the most bones is the winner.

Snake Sting

Equipment: 1 rope.

The Pack stand in a circle. One Cub outside the circle is Kaa, the snake, who walks round trailing the rope. Kaa taps someone on the back and then runs round as fast as he can. The Cub who has been stung runs after him trying to catch his tail. If Kaa gets to the vacant place before the tail is caught, he still remains Kaa. The tail must always be caught by the hands and not trodden on.

Mowgli, Where are you?

Equipment: Blindfold; roll of newspaper.

The Cubs sit in a circle and the leader chooses two of them to go into the centre. One is Mowgli and the other Baloo. Baloo is given the roll of newspaper and blindfolded. He calls, 'Mowgli, where are you?', and Mowgli replies from within the circle, 'Here I am, Baloo!'

Baloo listens to the direction of the voice and tries to hit Mowgli once with the newspaper. If he catches Mowgli, the Cubs change roles. But if after six attempts he still has not caught him, then he goes back to the circle and another Baloo is chosen.

General

Spot the Errors

Equipment: Pencil and paper per Six.

The leader tells a story, purposely making mistakes. The subjects could be Health Rules—Highway Code—Country Code. When the story is finished, the Cubs go to their Six corners and list the errors. The Six who notices the most is the winner.

Criss-Cross Quiz

Preparation: Set out 9 chairs in 3 rows of 3. Prepare a list of questions on the Arrow Tests.

The Cubs line up in two teams. One team with their caps on, and the other with their caps off. They are Noughts and Crosses.

The Cubs in each team are asked a question in turn. If a Cub answers correctly he sits on the chair of his choice. If he is wrong, he goes to the end of his team and the question passes to the other side. The first team with a completed line of Noughts or Crosses wins.

Note: Teams of six a side are large enough. Most Packs will need to run two games simultaneously.

Fishing for Tests

This is a good game for revision.

Equipment: 1 fishing rod with magnet attached for each Six; a set of cards, 1 card for every Cub in the Pack; scissors; paints or crayons; paper clips.
Preparation: This may be done during a handicraft session. The shape of a fish is drawn on each of the cards and then painted or coloured by the Cubs. On the plain side, a Test Activity is written for one, two or several Cubs, e.g. fold and hoist the Union Flag (2 Cubs), bandage an ankle (2 Cubs), tie a sheet bend (1 Cub).

One Cub from each Six is sent out with the rod to fish, he brings back his catch and starts his activity, if necessary asking another Cub to join him.

Meanwhile another boy goes fishing until the whole Six is occupied. As each activity is completed it is presented to the leader who awards points. Then the Cub may go and fish again.

Cubs catching a task they cannot perform or which is beyond their Arrow Test stage, may pass it to another member of the Six and await their turn to fish again.

Arrow Test

Whistle Stop

This is another good revision game.

Equipment: A packet of sweets; a plate; a whistle.

The Pack sit in a circle. A plate of sweets is passed round. When the leader blows the whistle the Cub holding the plate is asked a question on the Arrow Tests. If he answers correctly, he may take a sweet. If he is wrong, he hands a sweet to the Cubs sitting on either side of him and then passes the plate on.

Note: This could be played with questions on the District in which the Pack lives.

Something Good to Eat

Equipment: 1 beanbag; 3 beans or tokens per Cub.

The Cubs sit in a circle, one boy in the centre holds the beanbag. The leader calls out a letter and the Cub in the centre throws the beanbag to any player. He must name something good to eat beginning with that letter before the Cub in the centre counts to 20. If he fails, or mentions something already used, he surrenders a bean.

Musical Parcel

Equipment: Tape recorder or record player with music; wrapping paper; string or elastic bands; a list of Arrow Test questions.
Preparation: Parcel up an old book with plenty of layers of wrapping paper.

Write the test questions out on slips of paper and put each slip between a layer of wrapping paper. The Cubs sit in a circle in Six order and the leader hands them the parcel which they pass round to the music. When the music stops, the Cub holding the parcel unwraps one layer of paper and finds a question. If he answers it correctly, he gains two points for his Six.

If he cannot answer but another member of his Six can, then that Cub gains one point.

It is not practicable to offer the questions to other Sixes, the answer is usually a simultaneous shout, followed by heated assertions of priority!

Note: Make sure that the Sixes get equal turns.

Snakes and Ladders

Equipment: A board or a large sheet of paper; a dice; counters.
Preparation: Prepare the board as for Snakes and Ladders. Each Snake and Ladder should be numbered to correspond with a list of statements at the side of the board. The statement will be based on Health Rules, e.g.:

1. A ladder, 'I washed my hands before tea.'
2. A snake, 'I did not brush my teeth before going to bed.'

A group of Cubs learning Health Rules can play this with their leader who can slip a little pointed instruction as each snake or ladder is encountered. A lot of instructions can thus be given without the need of a formal talk.

The Rival Chefs

Equipment: A variety of food advertisements cut out from magazines; 1 paper bag for each Six; 1 piece of paper; 1 crayon.

Each Six collects a paper bag full of advertisements. They give themselves the name of a cafe or restaurant and prepare their 'Meal of the Day' menu which they print in crayon on a piece of paper.

The Six with the most sensible and attractive meal is the winner.

The Right Foods to Eat

Equipment: Pictures of food cut from magazines, including those that are fattening, bad for the teeth, etc.
The Cubs could be asked to bring the pictures themselves and points could be awarded to the Six who collect the most.
Preparation: Place the pictures around the room, some can be half hidden.

The Pack line up in Sixes and one Cub for each Six sets off in turn to find something to eat. The leader should set a time limit on the search, which slows down as the pieces become more difficult to find.

As the Sixes collect the foodstuffs, they place them in three groups:

1. Food that is good for us.
2. Food which makes us fat.
3. Food which is bad for our teeth.

Health

Cleanliness   Bronze

The Cubs sit in the Pack circle and each Cub is given a particular action from the cleanliness rules, e.g. wash your hands, brush your teeth, etc. The leader tells a story incorporating the actions concerned and when any of these are mentioned the Cubs run round the outside of the circle and back to their places. The first one home gains a point for his Six, but only if he can demonstrate the action to the leader's satisfaction.

After every Cub has had one turn, the game may be varied. The leader will tell another story in which the Cubs will run round the circle as soon as they think any activity mentioned makes one of their actions necessary, e.g. someone fetches in the coal—wash your hands; someone has dinner—brush your teeth.

Health Ladder   Bronze

Equipment: For each Six: 1 large white card (foolscap size); a set of small cards (half postcards); 1 counter; 1 felt-tipped pen with broad nib.
Preparation: Draw a ladder on each of the large cards leaving at least $\frac{3}{4}$ in. between rungs. On each of the small cards write a statement based on a health rule, e.g. took an apple to school to eat after lunch —go up three; ate a sweet in bed after cleaning teeth—go down four. Place a ladder, a set of cards and a counter in front of each Six.

Note: The number of 'ups' and 'downs' must be the same in each set, although the health rules need not be the same. Make sure that the first card in the set is an 'up'.

At the word 'Go!' the first Cub runs up, picks up a card, reads the statement aloud and moves his counter accordingly. The rest of the Six follow in turn until either the cards are finished or a Six gets to the top of a ladder. The cards can then be shuffled and given to different Sixes, for another round.

Mouse behind Curtain   Silver

The Cubs line up at the end of the hall. The leader stands at the other end with her back to them.

The Cubs creep up slowly (heel-to-toe steps) behind her.

The leader turns round suddenly and catches those moving. Those caught may keep their places if they can answer a health rule question correctly. If they fail, they must go back and start again. The winner is the one to touch the leader first.

Health Box   Gold

The Cubs sit in a circle with the leader who starts by saying, 'In my health box—I put some elastoplast.'

The next Cub continues, 'In my health box I put—some elastoplast and some cotton wool.'

So it goes on round the circle, including simple First Aid requirements such as prepared sterile dressings, antiseptic cream, etc.

First Aid Message   Gold

The Pack line up in Sixes with about 2 metres (2 yds.) space in between each boy.

The Seconds run up to the leader who whispers a message which will involve dealing with an emergency.

The Seconds return to their Sixes and pass the message on to the Cub in front, and so on through the Six until it reaches the Sixer who is standing at the back. He acts on the message, organizing his Six to deal with the emergency.

The leader should allow five minutes preparation time before asking each Six to act their sketch, in turn. The discrepancies are revealing and amusing.

Feats of Skill

Electric Touch   Bronze

Equipment: 1 ball per Six.

A mountaineer has been climbing all day and arrives exhausted at a chalet. There is food but unfortunately the electricity supply is a little uncertain, and needs looking after—this is where the Cub Pack can help.

The Pack line up in their Sixes and number off one to six. Then they must stand in the chalet to connect the current of the electricity like this: 6 5 4 3 -2 -1

With a space between numbers 1, 2 and 3. Number 3 holds the ball which is the current of electricity.

When the leader gives the signal, number 3 throws the ball to 2 who catches it, turns round and throws it to 1. Number 1 then runs with the ball to the back of the team and hands it to number 6 who passes it to 5, he gives it to 4 who is now at the head of the team, numbers 2 and 3 having moved up a place, so the formation is now:

1 6 5 4 -3 -2

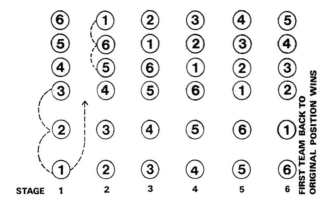

The same ball-throwing exercise is repeated remembering that the ball must be caught each time, passing through each pair of hands— or the electricity will fail. This carries on until the team is back in the starting position with number 3 holding the ball in the air to show that they have finished.

Ball Throwing   Bronze

Equipment: 1 ball per Six.

The Cubs line up in their Sixes with the newest and youngest in front for the shorter throws.

Each Sixer is given a ball and comes to the front of the Six. He throws the ball to the first Cub who returns it and squats down, then to the second boy who does the same and so on until the last Cub. He catches it, returns it to the Sixer and sits down. Then he stands again ready for the second throw and catch with the Sixer.

Discovering Nature

Zoo Escapes

Equipment: Pictures of birds, enough for twice the number of Cubs in the Pack; the same number of small cards.

Preparation : This game is better played out of doors or in a large hall. Write the names of the birds on the cards. All the birds in the Zoo have escaped, their labels are there but the Zoo 'keepers' want them caught and renamed.

The Pack divides in half. One group are the 'keepers' and the other half the escaped birds. The birds wear their names. When one is caught, it is brought to the table where the pictures are displayed. The 'keeper' has to find the picture of the bird he has captured, and take both to the leader.

If he is right, the 'keeper' wins a point and the 'bird' is given another name. If the 'keeper' selects the wrong picture, the 'bird' stays free and the picture is returned, to the table.

Note: A variation—if the 'keeper' identifies the 'bird' correctly, he may change roles with the 'bird'.

I Spy Bronze

Equipment: I Spy or similar Nature Book; counters.

The leader selects a bird, tree or animal from the book and reads out snatches of information about it. When a Cub thinks he recognises the description he calls out the name. If wrong, he may not try again until the others in the group have all had a guess. Then the leader starts another description.

Wildlife Spotting Bronze

Equipment: Pictures of birds, native wild animals, butterflies, etc. pencil and paper per Six.
Preparation: Number the pictures and place them around the room. List the numbers on the pieces of paper.

The room is an island where no one molests the wild life, but where observers are welcome. The Pack arrives by boat and tiptoes around the room, each Six making a list of the creatures spotted.
No one may touch a picture and marks are lost for making a noise. At a given signal, all return to the boat and points are given for the creatures correctly named.

Nature Snap
Bronze

Equipment: An old pack of playing cards; paste.
Preparation: Find pictures of animals, flowers, birds, etc., to make a
set of Snap cards. Allow four pictures for each example. They need
not be identical but must be easily recognisable as the same species,
and of a size which can be pasted on to an old pack of playing cards.
Cubs learning their Bronze Arrow Nature Test can prepare the cards
one week and play the game the following week.

When playing Snap, the Cubs must be able to name the item they
snap, in order to claim the cards.

Constellation Jigsaw
Gold

Equipment: 4 sheets of black paper 20 × 15 cm. (8 × 6 in.) per Six;
1 white crayon; 2 packets of silver stars.
Preparation: Draw a wavy line across each sheet dividing it in half.
On the upper half stick the stars on the paper in the shape of a con-
stellation. On the bottom half write the name of each constellation.
Cut in half and give the top halves to the Sixes. One complete set
of each constellation is needed for each Six.

The bottom halves are shuffled and placed in the centre of the room.
The Cubs sit in their corners and in turn run up to the centre of the
room and find the name of the constellation called by the leader. At
first the Cubs will go by shape of the jigsaw but gradually they will
learn the constellation itself.

**Note: If a few extra jigsaw pieces are made there will be a
selection to choose from even for the last Cub.**

Wildlife Spotting for Older Cubs

Equipment: Pencil and paper per Cub; collection of bird pictures, 2
of each bird.
Preparation: One set of pictures should be numbered only and
placed down one side of the room in numerical order. The second set
should be named and placed down the far side in a different order
from the first.

List the numbers on the Cubs' papers before they begin. The Cubs
look first at the numbered birds and write down the names of any
birds they know against the numbers on their papers. For the names
they do not know they search among the named pictures opposite,
checking for similarities.
   This is an excellent exercise in observation.

Safety

Highway Code Pairs   Bronze

Equipment: 2 sets of cards.
Preparation: Paste on to one set some illustration of traffic signs. On the other set write the corresponding description.

The cards of both sets are jumbled up and then placed face down. The first Cub turns up two cards which probably do not pair up. Everyone notes what they are, and he turns them down again. Should they be a pair he takes them and has another turn.

As the game progresses memory plays a bigger part, so it is important that none of the positions should be changed.

This game may be played with other designs—e.g. nature pictures, flags, mapping signs.

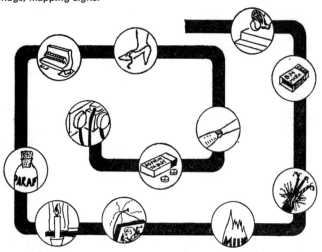

Home Safety Trail   Bronze

Equipment: A number of articles which could be a danger in the home; pencil and paper per Six.
Preparation: Lay a trail around the room of things which could cause accidents, e.g. aspirin tablets, frayed flex on an electric fire, matches, etc.

The leader describes to the Pack the people who live in the house—a toddler, Granny and so on.

The Cubs go round the trail in Sixes assessing the dangers which they write down and afterwards read out.

Home Safety Jigsaw   Bronze

*Equipment: ROSPA (Royal Society for the Prevention of Accidents)
Home Safety Picture, 'Careless Cottage' for each Six.*
*Preparation: Paste the picture on to strong cardboard or three-ply
wood and cut into a jigsaw, making each danger in the home the
subject one of the pieces of each jigsaw.*

Place the pieces face down in a pile in front of each Six. The first
Cubs from each Six run to their pile and select a piece. When they
can tell the leader what the danger is, they may carry the piece back
to their Six and the next boy runs up.

The Six with the first complete jigsaw is the winner.

Service

Emergency Calls

Equipment: An old or a toy telephone.

The Cubs form a large circle in Six order and number off, 1 to 6.

The leader puts the telephone in the middle and announces an
emergency, e.g. 'There is a fire at the Supermarket at the corner of the
High Street and Turners Lane.'

Then the leader calls out a number and the Cubs with that number
run round the circle, back through their places and into the centre.
The first Cub to reach the telephone dials 999. The leader acting as
the operator asks which service he requires. The Cub replies Fire,
Police or Ambulance, and when through, reports correctly the emergency and its location.

Flags and Countries

National Anthem Happy Families   Bronze

Equipment: A set of cards, 1 per Cub.
*Preparation: Write a line of the National Anthem on each of the
cards.*

The leader gives each Cub a card and they must find the other Cubs
who have the lines necessary to complete their verse of the National
Anthem. The first group of Cubs to complete a verse are the winners.

**Note: In order to complete a verse it will probably be
necessary for Assistants to join in the game.**

Union Flag Castles
Silver

Equipment: A set of Union Flag Cards as supplied by The Scout Shop—1 per Cub, or more as desired; counters—enough for 1½ times the number of Cubs in the Pack.
Preparation: Arrange chairs in a square in the centre of the room, leaving an entrance to each corner. Distribute the cards around the room.

Each entrance in the square is a gate, one each for England, Ireland, Scotland and Wales. When the leader calls 'Enter by England's gate', the Cubs run and collect a card depicting an English emblem, saint or flag and show it to the leader. If the card is correct he admits them to the castle, while his assistant gives them a counter. They then go out of the castle and the leader calls 'Gate is closed' and moves to another entrance. The cards are put around the room again by an assistant while the next gate is being called out. The winner is the Cub with the most counters.

Climb the Flagpole
Silver

Equipment: 1 large piece of (foolscap size) card per Six; 1 dice per Six; 1 counter per Cub.

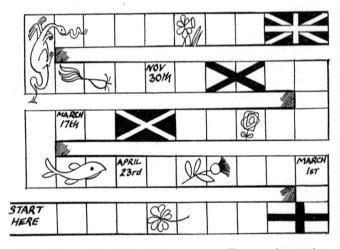

Each Six has a card, a dice and some counters. The game is a version of Snakes and Ladders. Each time a Cub lands on an illustrated square, he must say what it represents. If he is correct he may stay there; if not, he must move back a square. The aim is to see which Six can reach the top of the Flagpole first.

Flag Emblem Relay Silver

Equipment: A set of large (quarto size) white cards, 1 card per Six; crayons; felt-tipped pen.
Preparation: On one side of each draw a large illustration of one of the flags of the British Isles, covering the whole card. Colour this appropriately. Turn the card over, divide the other side into four squares. Each square being subdivided diagonally. Here is an example of how each section should be set out:

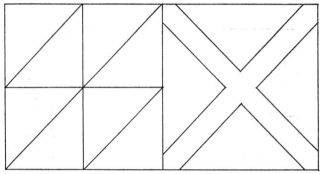

Front face of card   **Reverse face**

There is a natural progression between each square, so that when they are cut out the game will be a relay.

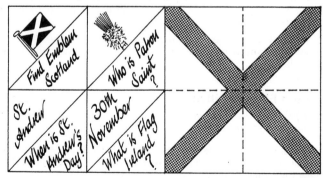

All the cards are then jumbled up and placed upwards at the end of the hall. Each Sixer is given a card which begins with a flag. He runs to the cards and selects the answer, which he takes back to his Six. The next Cub runs up to find the answer to that card and so on, until the cards form a large flag when turned over. The cards are then jumbled up again and each Six is given a different flag.

Flag Dominoes Silver

*Equipment: A set of flag and emblem cards from The Scout Shop,
roughly 1 per Cub, but so there are 2 of each kind; the same number
of small cards.*
*Preparation: Cut out each flag, emblem or saint and paste an
assorted pair on to a card like a domino.*

The leader distributes the cards to the Sixes. The first Six lays a card
in the centre of the room and the next Six must match it at either end.

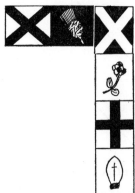

If the Six cannot match, they must 'knock' and the game will pass
on to the next Six. The first Six to clear all its dominoes is the winner.
That Six gains ten points.

Note: As each Cub places his domino, he must say what the
'match' is and if he says this correctly, he gains a point for
his Six.

Union Flag Families Silver

*Equipment: Union Flag and Emblem cards as supplied by The Scout
Shop; counters or tokens.*

The Cubs sit in a circle with their hands behind their backs. The
leader places a card in the hands of each Cub, being careful to give
new Cubs simple cards.

When the leader calls 'Go!' the Cubs look at their card and call out
the country it belongs to. The first country to get together and sit on
the floor is the winner.

Winners may be given a token and the game is repeated. At the
end of the game the Cubs return to their Six corners and add up their
tokens.

Knotting

The Longest Rope   Silver

Equipment: 1 rope per Six, all being the same length; a collection of old rope lengths, roughly 5 per Six; score board.

Each Six is given one of the ropes of equal lengths. The other ropes are placed in a pile in the centre of the room.

When the leader calls 'Go!' one Cub from each Six runs to the centre pile and selects a rope which he takes back to his corner. That rope must be tied to the Six rope before another one can be fetched from the pile. When there are no more ropes, the leader and his assistant go round to check the knots and a score for each Six is chalked up on the score board.

10 points are given for the longest rope in the Pack.
5 points for second longest.
5 points are given for each knot correctly tied.

Yachting Race   Gold

Equipment: 2 ropes per Cub—preferably 1 rope and 1 cord.

The Cubs form a wide circle round the room with all the ropes lying in the centre. The circle starts to move. The leader will use nautical terms as orders:

'Sail'—walk.
'Tide Racing'—run.
'Come About'—while running the cubs about turn, ducking and shouting.
'Lee O'—still running and ducking as they do so, because the boom is coming across.

Interspersed with these orders will be others referring to knots:

'Join Ropes'—Reef knot.
'Secure Sheet'—Sheet bend.
'Make Fast'—Round Turn and Two Half Hitches.
'Man Overboard'—Bowline round himself.

At these orders all stop and those who think they know the knot, grab a rope from the centre, tie the knot required and take it to the leader. If the knot is correct, the Cub gains a mark for his Six.

The Cubs who do not know the knots call 'Drop Anchor' and sit on the floor where they are.

Arrow Test

After a couple of minutes to tie knots, the leader says 'Up Anchor'. They then untie knots, drop ropes and return to the circle. Those who dropped anchor stand at the order 'sail'. The circle is off again.

Six Knotting Relay   Gold

Equipment: 1 rope for each Cub; a list of knots, 1 for each Six.
Preparation: A short revision of knots with leaders before starting the game.

The leader gives each Sixer a list of knots. The Sixer then decides which Cub will do each knot. The leader calls out a knot and the appropriate Cub runs up from each Six and does the knot as quickly as he can. The first to finish gets 4 points for his Six, the second gets 3 and so on. The winning Six is that with the most points.

Help! Help!   Gold

Equipment: 1 rope per Cub; piece of chalk.
Preparation: Draw a line at either end of the room. One marks the shore and the other a sandbank—with the sea in between.

One Cub from each Six is stranded on the sandbank and shouts for help. The rest of the Cubs in each Six are lined up on the shore, each carrying a rope. On the word 'Go !' they join their ropes together with a sheet bend. The Sixer ties a bowline around himself and the other end of the rope is attached to a 'tree' with a round turn and two half hitches. Before setting off on the rescue all the knots must be checked by a 'life-guard'—the leader or one of his assistants. When they are all correct, the Sixer swims to a sandbank and ties a rope around the stranded Cub, who is hauled to the shore. The line is then thrown out to the Sixer, who ties a bowline around himself and is pulled ashore.

Note: It is essential that the knots are checked quickly so this is an occasion when members of the Troop could be co-opted to help.

Knotting Market   Gold

Equipment: 1 thick and 1 thin rope per Cub; 3 counters per Cub.

The leader distributes the rope to each Cub. When he calls 'Go !' the Cubs may do any knot and bring it to show the leader. If it is correct, the Cub receives a counter, judging each Cub's effort by his Arrow Test standard. The Cubs continue to do the knots until time is up, but no Cub may do the same knot twice running. The Six with the most counters is the winner.

International Games

These games come from all over the world, although some may sound familiar.

Tell the Cubs where the games come from, and ask them what they know about the country. Pool the knowledge from the Pack and add some facts yourself. This will give the Cubs a background to the game.

This could become a regular weekly feature. When starting a new International Game, ask the Pack about the last one and see if they can remember something about the game and something about the country.

These games may be connected with the Gold Arrow Test—'Flags and Countries'.

Targets
Finland

Equipment: A piece of white card for each Cub (approximately quarto size), cardboard box lids are useful for this; enough paper for Cubs to make 3 darts; crayons; chalk; scissors; string.

Preparation: This would be ideal for a handcraft session. Each Cub draws an animal on his card, colours it and cuts it out. He then makes 3 darts of his paper. Set up or hang up a number of the animals around the room, keeping some in reserve. Draw a chalk line a short distance before each target.

Each Cub may have three shots at an animal. If he scores a hit, he takes the animal and another is put in its place. The Cub may retrieve his darts and continue playing until the leader calls 'Stop!' and the Six with the greatest number of animals is the winner.

Fishes in the Sea
Belgium

Equipment: Several pieces of chalk.

The Cubs space themselves out round the room and all chalk a small circle around their feet. Each Cub is given the name of a fish. One Cub is chosen as the 'fisherman' and runs around the room calling the names of various fish. Those Cubs must leave their circles and follow him, copying any actions he does, to suggest the movement of the sea. Waving the arms, jumping up and down, etc. Suddenly he will shout 'The sea is rough!' and all the fish and the 'fisherman' dash for a circle. But as the 'fisherman' did not originally have a circle, one Cub will be out. He then becomes the next 'fisherman'.

Hanging out the Washing
Holland

Equipment: For each Six: 1 rope; 1 newspaper; 2 clothes pegs per Cub.

The leader gives each Six a rope, supply of newspaper and clothes pegs. The Six hang up their clothes line in the Six corner and each Cub tears a garment shape out of the newspaper which they hang on the line. The leader awards points for the best garments and the Six who finish first.

Brothers
U.S.A.

The Cubs all find a partner and stand in a circle. One Cub faces inwards and his partner outwards, so that two circles are formed.

When the leader calls 'Go!' the two circles run round in opposite directions until the leader calls 'Brothers'. The Cubs then have to find their partner, hold hands and squat on the floor. The last pair down are out, but they remain sitting as part of the circle, the other Cubs running outside them. This keeps the circle large and the game more exciting.

St. George and the Dragon   Australia

Equipment: 2 pieces of wool per Cub.

The Cubs get into groups of three. One of the Cubs is 'St. George' and he ties a piece of wool loosely round each arm. The other two Cubs are the 'Dragon', one Cub is the head and the other holding on to his waist is the tail. The tail Cub also wears a piece of wool on each arm.

St. George tries to kill the Dragon by detaching the wool from his tail. When one piece of wool is gone, he is wounded; when both are gone, he is dead. At the same time the Dragon has to get the wool from St. George. When one of them is killed, the whole Pack stop and a new St. George is chosen for each group.

Compass Game   Sweden

Equipment: 1 (quarto size) card per Six; 1 long pencil per Six.
Preparation: Mark the cards with crosses as for the points of a com-
pass, but only name North.

The Pack line up in Sixes and the cards are placed opposite each Six
at the far end of the room. The pencil is placed on the card like the
needle of a compass, pointing to the North.

The leader calls out a compass bearing. The first Cub runs to the
card and places the pencil as he thinks correct. If he is right, he may
stand behind the compass. If he is wrong, he returns to the back of
his Six. The game continues until one Six has all its members behind
the compass.

The Postman and the Robbers   Sweden

Swedish Cubs play this game on skates.

Equipment: 3 newspapers; roll of sticky tape.
Preparation: Cut the newspapers into strips and make each into a
band by sticking both ends of the strips together.

Half the Pack are 'Postmen' and wear the paper bands, slung
diagonally over one shoulder. The other half are 'Robbers'.

When the leader calls 'Go !' the 'Robbers' try to catch the 'Postmen'
by breaking off their paper bands. A 'Postman' may return to base to
get another band. The 'Robber' who collected the most post is the
winner. Then the 'Postmen' and the 'Robbers' change places.

International

Grab
France

Equipment: 1 article for each Cub (less 1)—balls, beanbags, etc.

The Cubs line up at one end of the room and the articles are placed at the other end. The leader gives the Cubs a series of directions, e.g. take a pace forward, turn about, hop on one foot, etc. Until he calls 'Grab!' and the Cubs make a rush for the articles. One boy will be out and he may sit behind the articles, while the leader removes an article each time, until finally the winner is found.

Whirlwinds
Mauritius

Two boys start as whirlwinds, joining hands and trying to catch another boy. As in chain 'HE' each boy caught joins on until there are six, when the whirlwind divides into two. As each whirlwind reaches six boys, it breaks again. The winner is the Cub who eludes capture the longest.

Hail O King!
Israel

The leader chooses one Cub as the 'King' and he sits on his 'throne' at the top of the room. Each Six goes to its corner and the Cubs plan an action which they can mime, e.g. gardening.

The Sixes then gather round the 'King'. He addresses one of the Sixes and asks, 'Where have you been?', and the Six reply, 'Far away in the forest.'

The 'King' then asks, 'What have you been doing?', and the Six mime its action. The 'King' tries to guess what the Cubs are doing. When he succeeds he gives chase and the Six must run to the farthest wall of the room. The 'King' asks each Six in turn and the one with the least Cubs caught by the 'King' is the winner.

Hands on Land   Denmark

Equipment: A long rope, enough to make a large circle for the Cubs to sit round.

The Cubs sit outside the rope circle which is a lake. When the leader calls 'Hands in water!' all the Cubs put their hands in the lake. When he calls 'Hands on land!' all the Cubs put their hands outside the rope.

At the command 'Hands on bank!' the Cubs put their hands on the rope. The last to move is out. The game can be made increasingly difficult by the leader saying—'Hands on water!' or 'Hands in land!' or just 'In water' or 'On land', when no one should move.

Acting Games

Imaginative play and acting come naturally to children of Cub Scout age. Acting games are a simple means of giving Cubs an opportunity for self-expression. The quick bit of acting in a game helps the shy new Cub to find his feet, and the boy who is not a success in athletic activities may well shine in an acting game.

The game which involves speaking helps a boy to gain confidence in using his voice and there are opportunities for the 'show off' to direct his self-importance into a worthwhile channel.

Acting games are, of course, a great opportunity for the 'family' type of activity.

What is my Job?

The Cubs line up in Six formation at one end of the hall and the Sixers walk to the other end and stand facing them. Each Six decides on a job of work which they will mime, e.g. sweeping a path, drilling a hole in the road. They then walk up towards the Sixer saying, 'There came a man across the common to do a job of work'. The Sixer says, 'What job?' and the Cubs reply, 'Any old job'.

The Sixer replies, 'Then set to work and do it'. The Cubs perform their actions and the Sixer tries to guess their job. When he guesses correctly he gives chase. Any Cub that he catches joins him for the next game.

Who am I?

Equipment: A list of occupations that may be mimed, e.g. barber.

The Cubs sit in their Six corners. One Cub from each Six goes to the leader who gives them an occupation. The Cubs go to their corners and mime the occupation to the rest of their Six. When they have guessed correctly, the next Cub goes to the leader, gives him the answer and is in turn given the next occupation on the list. The first Six to reach the end of the list is the winner.

The Queen's Highway

An activity for a special Pack Meeting.

Equipment: Chalk; large sheets of white card; 3 sets of red, yellow and green balloons; poster paints or crayons.
Preparation: This could ideally be reserved for a handcraft section. The cards are cut up and painted as various road signs. When all the equipment has been prepared the road is chalked round the room with zebra crossings, parked vehicles, bends, crossroads and various other obstructions and cautions. The road signs should be propped up on chairs at various stages along the route, and at one point the assistant will stand at the traffic lights holding a red, yellow and green balloon.

Each Cub chooses a character—mother with a pram, an old lady, a car, a lorry, a bus—then in turn each Six will go from one end of the course to the other observing correctly all the cautions and signs. At the end the leader will award points for the correct procedure to each Six.

Note: Several judges will be necessary to observe the Cubs and award the points. This is a possible activity for a special Pack Meeting.

Acting

Running Commentaries

The leader decides on a story with plenty of action and character. He picks several Cubs to play the leading characters but the whole Pack must join in the acting of the story either as a crowd or a vehicle such as a boat or train, e.g. if a boat is needed, a long line of Cubs can sit on the floor, facing one who is the 'stroke', and when a voyage is mentioned, they move backwards and forwards as though rowing, each Cub holding on to the shoulders of the one in front.

The sort of story which is ideal is 'The story of St. Patrick'. The leader is the commentator and Cubs are chosen to represent St. Patrick, his parents, Mithcu—the Irish Chieftain, pirates, a boat and a group of Irish people.

The leader tells the story of Patrick's life as a boy in Wales, the arrival of the pirate boat and the kidnapping of the boy. Next comes his life in Ireland as the slave of Mithcu, his escape after a long but weary journey, his return home, his years of study and his return to Ireland as a Bishop. The story may end with St. Patrick surrounded by the Irish people, plucking the shamrock and showing it to them, and finally with the people kneeling around him.

The leader can divide the story into scenes or pass from one incident to another with the Cubs acting each scene. It is important, however, that every Cub should be involved.

Dumb Man's Sing Song

Equipment: A slip of paper per Cub; Akela's hat.

The Pack sit in a circle and the leader gives each Cub a slip of paper. The Cubs write on their slip the name of their favourite camp-fire song. The leader chooses two of the Cubs as 'Dumb Men' and having collected the slips of paper and jumbled them up in the hat, one of the 'Dumb Men' draws out a slip. The two Cubs then mime the song and when the Pack have guessed, they start to sing it.

Miming to Sound

Equipment: 1 tape recorder.
Preparation: Record a number of sounds, e.g. a tap dripping, a kettle whistling, a passing car—or to be more adventurous the shaking of rice or beans in a tin, or the crunching of a P.V.C. mackintosh. You can experiment with all manner of ordinary things like saucepan lids, tin and paper. Be careful to watch the sound level and do not make the sounds too near the microphone. When recording each group of sounds you should have some kind of story in mind so that the sounds have a composition; e.g. if the sounds are weird it may be a space story or a thriller, if they are household noises it could be a comedy.

The Pack sit in a circle and the leader plays back the group of sounds for each Six. Once the Pack have heard all the sounds they go back to their corners and work out a story to mime around the sounds. After three minutes practice time all the Cubs sit in the circle and the leader will then choose the first Six to mime to their sounds.

Note: This game is rather like a version of Kim's Game, as much depends on each Six remembering the sounds that were allotted to them.

What Am I Doing?

Equipment: 1 broomstick; 1 whistle.

The Pack form a circle and pass round the broomstick. When the leader blows the whistle, the Cub holding the broomstick has to act with it, e.g. using it as a fishing rod, sword or even a hair brush ! If the Cubs act something which has been done before, they pay a forfeit.

A variation on this game is:

What Next?

Equipment: For each Six a set of different articles, e.g., 1 scrubbing brush; 1 bag; 1 frying pan; 1 ruler.

Each Six line up with their set of articles in front of them. The leader asks the first Cub in each Six to pick up their first article and use it as something else, e.g. a frying pan, as a banjo. Then the second Cub picks the next article and so on, until gradually the Cubs run out of ideas.

Acting

Famous Hats

Equipment: A supply of newspaper; some gummed strip paper.

The leader gives each Cub some newspaper and gummed strip paper and they make a hat of a famous person, real or fictitious. When every Cub has made a hat, the leader asks each, in turn, to act their character, and the rest of the Pack must guess who they are.

Shopping Bag

Equipment: 1 large shopping bag; 1 whistle.

The Pack is seated in a circle and the shopping bag is passed round. When the leader blows the whistle the Cub holding the bag pretends to take something from it, e.g. comb. He then mimes the action of combing his hair and the rest of the Pack must guess what the article is.

Note: If the Cubs find it too difficult to think of articles, the leader can mention a variety of shops that the Cubs may have visited to stimulate the imagination.

Incident

Equipment: 3 cards per Six.
Preparation: Write on each of the cards an incident such as 'A boy is found lying unconscious beside his motor-bike', or 'A little girl is crying because she is lost'.

Each Six is given a card and is allowed five minutes to decide what they are going to do in their situation. Recognition should be given, to the Sixer who takes control, for the correct use of the telephone and for efforts to obtain adult help.

Noah's Ark

Equipment: 1 slip of paper per Cub.
Preparation: Write the names of animals on the slips of paper, reserving two slips for each animal.

The leader gives each Cub a slip. He explains that the Pack are all animals in Noah's Ark. There has been a great storm and each pair has got separated. Noah wants to try and pair the animals up again. So each Cub makes the noise of his animal and finds his partner.

As the animals are paired off they must go to the leader who is 'Mr. Noah' and act the animal they represent.

What do we see in our Town?

The leader tells the Pack a story bringing in the items listed below. As they are mentioned the Cubs form groups to portray each item.

1. A policeman—one Cub acts a policeman on point duty.
2. A church—two Cubs make a church with a steeple.
3. A tricycle—three Cubs make a man riding a tricycle.
4. Telephone box—four Cubs make a telephone box.
5. Fire engine—five Cubs make a fire engine.
6. A public meeting—six Cubs hold a public meeting.

Party Games

Party Games can be played at ordinary Pack meetings but it is more exciting for the Cubs if there are special games reserved for party time.

If there are any adults at the party they should be asked to join in, where possible pairing a Cub with an adult.

The more energetic games should not be played directly after eating, for you will have a lot of sick Cubs on your hands! Choose some games which can best be played as people are still arriving and make sure that your final game of the evening is one where everyone may join in.

A few inexpensive packets of sweets which can be shared among a winning Six add spice to the evening.

Chocolate Dice

Equipment: For each Six: 1 bar of chocolate; plate; knife; fork; dice; shaker; blindfold.

The Sixes sit in circles in their corners and take it in turn to throw the dice. The Cub who throws the first 6 is blindfolded and tries to eat the chocolate on the plate with the knife and fork. Meanwhile the other Cubs are trying to throw another 6, before the chocolate is devoured. When they do, the next Cub takes over.

Note: This is not a good game to play directly before or after tea and is best played either at the beginning of the party or right at the end.

Devil's Tail

A game suitable for Hallowe'en.

Equipment: 1 rope.

One Six is a 'devil'. The Cubs hang on, one behind the other, the last boy having a rope tucked into the top of his trousers and trailing on the ground.

The rest of the Pack make groups of three and link arms. They try to catch the 'devil' by treading on his tail. If the tail comes off, the 'devil' is finished. If the groups of three catching him break arms—they are finished. This continues until each Six has been the 'devil'.

Drawing a Prehistoric Monster

Equipment: 1 large sheet of paper per team; 2 or 3 crayons or felt-tipped pens per team.

The Pack divide into two teams and number off. The leader gives each Cub part of an animal to draw, but the parts must not run consecutively, e.g. number 1—eyes, number 2—tail.

In turn, each of the Cubs run up and draw their part for their team.

The completed drawings are finally put on show and judged for the best effort.

Happy Families

Equipment: Set of postcards, 1 per Cub; 1 felt-tipped pen.
Preparation: Divide the cards into sets of 5, or 4, according to the number of Cubs. Each set is a family and like the Happy Family cards there is a mother, father, sister, brother and baby. Draw their portrait on each card and write their names underneath, the funnier the better.

Party

The Pack sit on chairs in a circle and the leader gives each one a card. When he calls 'Go!' the Cubs swop cards until the leader tells them to stop.

Each Cub then calls out the name of his family and tries to find the other members. When the family is complete they sit together on a chair, father first, then mother, and brother, sister and last of all baby. The last family to sit on a chair have their cards taken away. When there is only one family left, they are the winners.

Cat and Mouse

Equipment: Whistle.

The Pack line up in 4 or 5 lines, each line of Cubs joining hands across. One Cub is chosen as 'Cat' and another as 'Mouse', the 'Cat' chases the Mouse up and down the lines.

When the leader blows the whistle the Cubs turn at right angles and form lines going down, by holding hands with the members of their new line. When the leader blows the whistle again the lines form across once more. When the 'Cat' has caught the 'Mouse' a new pair are chosen.

All Change

The Cubs sit in a circle on chairs. Three Cubs stand in the middle of the circle. They decide between themselves on something that will be common to a number of those in the circle and call this out, e.g. 'Everyone wearing a watch, change places!', thereupon all those wearing watches leap to their feet and change places. The three in the middle also endeavour to get a seat. The next three standing have to think of something else.

Note: Three boys in the centre will have fun, but one on his own can be very miserable.

Newspaper Hunt

Equipment: 1 newspaper per Six and 1 for the leader, the same edition and preferably one with several pages.

The leader gives each Six a newspaper which the Cubs take back to their corners. The Sixer divides the paper up, giving a page to each Cub. The leader looks at his newspaper and asks a question on one of the news items, e.g. 'Where did the Queen open a new Hospital?' The Cubs who have the answer take the paper to the leader and the first with the correct answer gains a point for his Six.

Filling Santa's Sack

Equipment: 1 balloon per Cub, with a few reserves; 1 sack per Six.

One Cub in each Six stands in his Six corner holding the sack. The leader spaces the rest of the Cubs out as far away from their Six corner as possible and gives each Cub a balloon. When the leader calls 'Go!' all the Cubs pat their balloon towards their Six corners and endeavour to get the balloon into the sack. The balloons may not be held in the hand and must be patted.

The first Six to get all their balloons into their sack is the winner.

Note: It is advisable to have different coloured balloons for each Six.

Balloon Football

Equipment: A good supply of balloons.

The Cubs form two teams and sit on the floor facing each other, their legs stretched out so that their feet almost touch those of the boy opposite. Two Cubs are chosen as goalkeepers and stand one behind each team. The leader throws a balloon into play and each team endeavours to pat the balloon over the heads of the opposing team. A goal is scored when the balloon touches the ground on the opponent's side. After a while the leader throws in a second balloon and then a third and the game becomes increasingly difficult. The team with the most goals is the winner.

Party

The Revolving Parcel

Equipment: 1 prize; 1 newspaper; 1 piece of brown paper; 1 piece of gay wrapping paper; roll of sticky tape; record player or tape recorder; record of light music.
Preparation: Wrap up the prize in some bright wrapping paper then in several layers of newspaper, two or three layers of brown paper and finally wrap the finished parcel in some gaily coloured wrapping paper.

The Pack sit in a circle and the leader starts the music. The Cubs pass the parcel around until the music stops. The Cub who is holding the parcel takes off one layer of paper. So the game goes on until a Cub takes off the last wrapping and wins the prize.

Mad Hatters

Equipment: 4 hats; 62 cm. (2 ft.) of elastic.
Preparation: Join the hats together with the elastic so that they may each be worn, but with difficulty.

The Pack divide into two teams. Within their teams the Cubs pair off, and sit side by side on chairs, parallel with the other team. At the top of the room, opposite each team are two chairs with the hats on. When the leader calls 'Go !', the first players in each team run to their chairs—pick up the hats—put them on. While they are doing this, the rest of their team moves up one, leaving the empty pair of chairs at the back of the team. The 'Mad Hatters' have to reach the back of their team and sit down. If a hat falls off they must stop to replace it. When they eventually reach their chairs, one of them runs back to replace the hat before the next player may start. The first team to complete is of course the winner.

Breathe In!

Equipment: 3 dozen dried peas; 2 saucers per Six; 1 drinking straw per Cub.

The Sixes line up in files with the two saucers in front of each. One saucer contains the dried peas, 12 or more, and the other is empty. The leader gives each Cub a drinking straw. When he calls 'Go!' the first Cub in each Six runs to his saucer and sucks one pea from the full saucer and drops it into the empty saucer, then runs to the back of his Six. If any fall on the floor they must remain there.

The leader counts the peas successfully transferred and declares the winners.

What is on Television?

Cut out a selection of programmes, illustrated if possible, from the Television magazines, number them and then obliterate the titles. Paste the programmes on cards and place them round the room. The Cubs try to identify the titles of the programmes and write them down.

Note: It is helpful to number the papers for the Cubs before they start, otherwise they are apt to write them down in a haphazard order, and get confused.

Hallo Sparrow!

The Cubs sit in a circle. The Cub to start says to his left-hand neighbour, 'Hallo, Sparrow, how art thee?'
Number 2 replies: 'Quite well, thankee, as thou canst see.'
Number 1: 'And how's thy neighbour next to thee?'
Number 2: 'I do not know, I'll ask and see.'
Number 2 then turns to Number 3.
Number 2 must choose another bird. The game progresses round the circle. If a bird is mentioned again, that Cub is out. The game continues until the birds are exhausted or one Cub is left victorious.
Encourage the use of a good rolling West Country accent!

Traps

A game which can be played with any number and a good one for adults to join in.

Equipment: Whistle.

Party

The adults join up in pairs to make arches. They stand in a circle, well spaced out and raise their joined hands to make the arches. The Cubs run round the circle under the arches. When the leader blows the whistle, the traps fall and the arches drop to catch a Cub. All those who are caught, join up to make arches until there is only one Cub left who is the winner.

Note: This is a dangerous game for boys with spectacles, so it is best if the adults ask these boys to be arches with them straight away. If this is done directly and unobtrusively the boys themselves will not guess the reason.

Rain Making

Another camp-fire game.

1. The leaves are rustling just before the rain starts. Just a whisper of sound—rub thumbs against first two fingers.
2. The first raindrops are pattering down. Rub palms of hands together slowly.
3. The rain is really falling now, cross your arms and rub your hands up and down on your arms as if you are cold.
4. Now the drops are bigger. Pat your knees with your hands as fast as you can.
5. Here comes the downpour. Tap your feet on the ground—very fast—but lightly. Then reverse the order until the rain stops.

Note: Perhaps more a camp fire stunt than a game—but good fun.

Memory Rhymes

The Pack divides into four groups seated round the campfire circle. The leader points to one of the groups who immediately starts to sing a nursery rhyme to the tune of 'Auld Lang Syne'. When this has been sung everyone sings to the same tune, the following chorus:

A—BCD—EFG—H
IJ—K—LM
NO—PQ—RS—TU
V—W—X—YZ.

The leader then points to another group, who sing another nursery rhyme to the same tune. The singing must be continuous, if a group pauses for more than three seconds they are out and any group repeating a nursery rhyme is also out.

Camp-fire Story

Equipment: A bag full of hats, gloves, scarves, etc.

The leader starts a story as the bag is passed round the camp-fire circle. When the leader pauses, the Cub holding the bag takes an article from it and continues the story bringing the article into it. The bag continues to be passed round while the story is being told. When the leader gives a signal the next Cub holding the bag takes an article and starts his story.

Expedition, Wide, and Field Games

Most active games are better played out of doors, but there are some games which need considerable space if they are to be enjoyed to the full. They come into their own when the Pack goes on an Expedition into the country and the Cubs have an opportunity to chase over a big field, a wonderful experience for a boy living in a flat in a large city. If you are lucky enough to have the right surroundings near your Headquarters of course, you can play them at any time. Nature Games are included in the Expedition section which use the resources of the countryside. The Sense Training section also has games on this theme. The Expedition is an opportunity for the Pack to have a complete change of programme, so make your games exciting and different too.

Wide Games—a Scouting term for the type of imaginative story game involving hunting, chasing and stalking. When playing a Wide Game with Cubs it is important to have a well-defined area, as an enthusiastic Cub can chase on and get lost in his excitement.

Field Games include some well-known versions of Cricket and Rounders. They are fast moving games, ideal for keeping warm in the cold weather.

On the Journey

Equipment: Pencil and paper per Six.

The Cubs try to spot something beginning with each letter of the alphabet. These must be written down in alphabetical order and nothing beginning with B may be spotted until A has been noted.

This can be played for general interest in one group, or competitively by a number of groups.

Note: One adult in each Six could do the job of writing.

Another Game for the Journey

Equipment: A supply of beans for scoring.
Preparation: Note down a list of things that could be spotted at intervals on the journey, e.g. Rolls-Royce, weather vane, etc.

The first Cub to spot one of the items is given a bean. That item is then eliminated and another added. The leader must have a good list ready, although ideas will no doubt occur as the journey proceeds.

Nature Dominoes

The leader gives each Six an identical specimen and they search for something similar, e.g. if the specimen is a clover leaf, they may find another leaf composed of three leaflets. If that is a blackberry leaf, the next item might be something which pricked—thistle and so on.

Each Six working separately make a chain of like to like and it is interesting to see how differently the Sixes develop their chains.

Nature Picture

Equipment: One sheet of drawing paper per Cub.

The leader gives each Cub a sheet of paper and they have to paint a picture, using only natural materials, e.g. blackberry juice, grass, etc.

Nature Alphabet

Each Six has to find a nature specimen for each letter of the alphabet. The leader should set a time limit.

Nature Zoo

Each Six builds a zoo of funny animals, using only natural materials.

Expedition

Nature Survey

Equipment: A length of rope about 4 metres (4 yds.) long for each Six.

Each Six makes a circle of their rope on a chosen piece of ground. Then the leader allows them five minutes to find as many things as possible in that circle.

Curio Collector

The leader makes a survey of the area and notes descriptive peculiarities such as trees struck by lightning, nuts gnawed by a squirrel, an animal's footprint. This could be done while the Pack are eating their lunch or tea. Then the leader tells the Pack of one of these curios and they set off to find it. When a Cub does find it, he calls the rest of the Pack and from there the leader sends them off to look for the next curio.

Note: This game may be developed as a trail.

At the end of the day

An excellent way of getting tired Cubs home cheerfully.

The leader gives the Pack the direction towards home or other destination. The Cubs run on ahead and hide by the time the leader has counted 10. The leader follows walking towards home.

The Cubs try to creep up behind the leader and touch him on the shoulder, without being spotted. When all the Pack have emerged, they run on and hide again. This is repeated until they reach their destination.

Hunt the Banderlog

Equipment: Sheets of stiff white paper; scissors.
Preparation: Cut out a large number of monkeys from the paper and hide them within a given area.

The only known collection of 'albino monkeys' have escaped from the local zoo and are known to be hiding in the area. A stockade has been built to hold the monkeys as they are recaptured. However, 'saboteurs' seem to be at work as the monkeys are disappearing as quickly as they are caught.

The Cubs scatter throughout the area and when they find a monkey they put it in the stockade. Meanwhile a pre-selected Six take each monkey out and hide it again. At the end of a given time the number of recaptured monkeys are counted, and all work together to round up any still at large.

Secret Rocket Planes

Equipment: 1 piece of wool per Cub; several large sheets of card; 1 felt-tipped pen; scissors; sticky tape.
Preparation: This may be done during a handcraft session. On each card draw the parts of an aeroplane, using sets of three parts to make up a plane complete with wings, fuselage and tail. These pieces must be drawn so that they fix together to make an actual plane:
Cut out:

Fig. 1 The fuselage

Cut slot for tail and wings

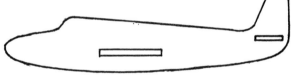

Fig. 2 The Wings

Fig. 3 The Tail

Wide

*Make enough plane parts for half the Pack, join one together as
shown below, but leave the rest for the Inventor.*
Join together:

Fig. 1

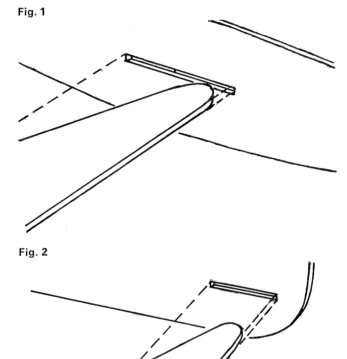

Fig. 2

Slide tail piece
into slot.

A shadow 'Factory' is turning out the parts for a new type of plane,
still on the secret list. These parts are then taken by specially chosen
messengers to the house of the 'Inventor', who is the only person
who knows how to assemble them. But a 'Foreign Power' has heard
rumours of what is going on and sends its spies to try and intercept
the parts en route. There are three essential parts which make up each
plane—wing section, fuselage and tail and the factory sends off these
parts continually throughout the game. The 'Inventor' builds as many

planes as possible with the parts given to him in the time limit of the game. At the same time the spies of the 'Foreign Power' endeavour to waylay the messengers, steal the parts and take them to their secret base to assemble their own planes.

The 'Factory' (the leader) and the 'Inventor' (an assistant) should be some two hundred yards apart in an area providing some cover. The 'Foreign Power' hideout being midway between them. A messenger cannot be caught while returning but if caught with a part on his journey to the 'Inventor', he must surrender it immediately and return to the 'Factory' for another one.

Messengers from the secret 'Factory' wear wool on their arms, the spies capture them by breaking the wool. The side with the greatest number of completed planes is the winner.

Note: Enough parts should be made out beforehand to last for half an hour.

Big Game Hunting

Equipment: A number of cards about 5 × 7·5 cm. (2 × 3 in.)—for a Pack of 24 at least 48 will be needed.

Preparation: Write the name of a wild animal on each card. Select an area of bushy or scrub land affording cover and with a central area or patch from which movement can be observed all round. Attach the cards to bushes in such a way that the Cubs can with care creep up and catch an animal. Dangerous animals such as lions and tigers should be in more exposed positions and therefore more difficult to catch.

The area is a game reserve in Africa. The leader is the 'Game Warden', and patrols the central area. The Cubs are 'Poachers' trying to catch the animals. They must start from an agreed base.

If the 'Warden' sees a 'Poacher', he calls out his name and points at him saying 'Bang! Bang!'.

The 'Poacher' has to return to base for treatment before hunting again. He may however keep any animals he has already caught. After fifteen minutes the Sixes add up their catches to see who has the most.

Sheep Rustlers

Equipment: Cotton wool; red powder paint; 2 colours of wool.

The Pack is divided into two parties, 'Sheep Rustlers' and 'Farmers'. They are identified by different colours of wool tied on their arms.

The 'Rustlers' have stolen the 'Farmer's' sheep in the night and set off for their hideout. On the way the sheep leave a trail of wool rubbed off on twigs, posts, etc. Some of the 'Rustlers' have been hurt and leave a trail of 'blood' (red powder paint).

After the 'Rustlers' have had a start, the 'Farmers' wake up, realise their sheep have been stolen and follow the trail of wool and blood. In due course the 'Rustlers' realise they are being followed and decide to find a good hideout for an ambush.

The excitement of the game is the fact that the 'Farmers' do not know at what point they will be ambushed. When the 'Farmers' arrive the 'Rustlers' spring out and a battle follows. Anyone with wool broken is dead. Finally a truce is declared and all agree to live peaceably.

Note: The leader following with the 'Farmers' should warn them that an ambush is likely and a battle will take place, otherwise some Cubs, taken by surprise may get too heated and the battle will be too realistic!

The Vanishing Postbox

This game should be played in a wooded area. A fast-moving game for a cold winter's day.

Equipment: Set of small cards, 4 per Cub; the same number of squares of gummed paper, a different colour for each Six; shoe box; crepe paper; sticky tape; scissors.
Preparation: Fasten the lid on to the shoe box with sticky tape then cover it with red crepe paper. Cut a large hole in the side to represent a post box. Write down the names of the Sixes and the colour of the stamps they are to have.

The leader is a 'Stationer' and his Assistants are respectively a 'Stamp Machine' and a 'Post Box'. The Cubs go to the 'Stationer' to buy a card, then to the 'Stamp Machine' where they say the name of their Six and get the correct colour stamps. They stick this on to the card and place it in the 'Post Box'.

Not as simple as it sounds! The 'Stationer', the 'Post Box' and the 'Stamp Machine' are all moving around in hiding. After ten minutes the leader calls the Pack together and they sort out the letters. The Six who has posted the most is the winner.

Note: It may be a good idea to have several 'Stamp Machines', one for each colour stamp.

Photographic Expedition

Equipment: Sets of pictures of animals, e.g. rabbits, squirrels, etc.— 6 or 7 is a suitable number; wool for 'lives'.

The leaders or extension Cubs are the 'Animals'. They take their sets of pictures and find a hiding-place within the specified area of the game.

The rest of the Pack are divided into 'Photographers' and 'Mosquitoes' in the ratio of approximately $\frac{2}{3}$: $\frac{1}{3}$.

The 'Photographers' set off to find and photograph the 'Animals'. If a 'Photographer' finds one he clicks and quickly takes a snap of it, then receives a picture from the 'Animal'. The object being to see how many he can photograph in a given time.

The 'Mosquitoes' who invade the forest try to sting the 'Photographers' by breaking the wool on their arms. If stung, a 'Photographer' must return to base for treatment and receive another life.

Note: Small boxes to represent cameras add to the fun of the game.

Stalking Kim's Game

Equipment: A collection of 25 different articles, which could be hung up with a piece of wool, e.g. pencil, rubber, etc., or if the Pack are at camp possible needs include some stones; wool for lives; pencil and paper per Six.
Preparation: Hang the articles on a bush, these must be of different sizes so that some may only be seen at very close range. They should also be arranged so that only a limited number may be seen from one position.

The Sixes are based at equal distances from the bush with pencil and paper. The leader guards the bush, walking slowly round while the Cubs creep up trying to identify the objects on the tree without being spotted by the leader. If seen they must return to base and try again.

They memorise the objects and after a given time the leader blows a whistle and all return to base where each Six make a list of the objects they have remembered.

The Swinging Jujus

Equipment: Wool for 'lives'; 2 ropes; material for making models of a crocodile and an alligator, e.g. logs, sacking, etc.

A juju is a symbol of man's superstitious nature and is a kind of mascot kept to ward off evil.

Two tribes in the jungle each have a juju displayed at the entrance to their village. One tribe has an 'Alligator' and the other a 'Crocodile' and these jujus are suspended from a tree outside the village about 1 metre (3 ft.) from the ground. Providing the jujus remain still, the tribes are safe, but should an enemy set them in motion every manner of ill fortune will befall.

Wide

The Pack divide themselves into the two tribes and set up camp about 200 metres (200 yds.) from each other. They make their jujus out of materials provided and any other natural materials they can find and suspend their mascots like giant pendulums.

Each tribe endeavours to set the other juju in motion, if a Cub succeeds in doing this, he gains five points for his team. But should the juju stop swinging before another strikes it, the first Cub will lose his points. Each tribe must have a 'Witch Doctor 'who keeps the score.

The tribes may defend themselves by stripping their attackers of the wool on their arms and then the attackers must return to their tribes for a fresh life. The winning tribe is the one with the least points scored against it at the end of the game.

Feeding The Grand Owl

Equipment: Wool for 'lives'.

An expedition has been made into darkest Africa by a party of ornithologists in search of an extraordinary bird known as the 'Grand Owl'. The zoo has offered a large sum for anyone who can bring back a specimen alive.

This bird is, however, held sacred by the natives and its capture therefore arouses great indignation.

Some half-mile of reasonably wooded country is chosen for the game and the 'Ornithologists' (half the Pack) have to see the 'Grand Owl' (the leader) safely through this, from the point of its capture at one end, to the zoo at the other end. The 'Ornithologists' have caged the bird securely and the natives realise that they stand no hope of retrieving it alive, but a peculiar fact about this owl is that unless it is fed at least once every five minutes it will die !

Throughout its journey, therefore, the 'Ornithologists' have continually to search for food for it. The type of food will depend upon the district: it may require one acorn every five minutes, or five beech leaves, or whatever is to be found in that particular country. So the 'Natives' agree that, rather than let it be taken alive to the zoo they will see that it dies of starvation on the way there!

The leader walks slowly through the woods and the 'Ornithologists' job is to see that he gets the necessary sustenance. The 'Natives' task is to put the Ornithologists out of action by breaking the wool on their arms, when the Ornithologists must return to the assistant at the beginning of the trail for a fresh life.

If five minutes elapse without any food reaching the 'Grand Owl', the bird gives a long dying whistle and the 'Natives' win the game. If it reaches the zoo safely, it gives three sharp whistles and the 'Ornithologists' win. The sides may then be reversed.

Palefaces and Indians

Equipment: Pieces of paper for secret messages.
Preparation: A 'different' supply is written on each piece of paper.

The Pack is divided into two parties. 'Palefaces' are trying to get supplies through to a besieged Fort. Each 'Paleface' carries something—a supply written on the piece of paper, which he hides about his person.

The 'Red Indians' stalk and catch the 'Palefaces' and search them for hidden supplies. When caught a 'Paleface' must stand still and count to 100, after which the 'Red Indian' must release him and he can proceed to the Fort. If his supplies are found he has to go back to collect some more.

Vital supplies must get through, if the Fort is to be relieved.

Huntsman and Hounds

Two homes are marked at either end of the game area and the 'Hares' wait in one of these. There is a 'Huntsman' and two or three 'hounds' who wear scarves on their heads to distinguish them. The 'Hares' rush across and try to get from one home to another without being caught by the 'Huntsman and Hounds'. If a 'Hound' catches a 'Hare' he must hold him down until the 'Huntsman' arrives to give three taps. The 'Hare' tries to escape and when tapped is killed.

When all are killed except one, that 'Hare' becomes 'Huntsman' and the last two or three, 'Hounds'.

Note: The 'Hares' try to get across the playing area as often as possible.

Star Trek Log Book

The Pack is divided into three groups. The 'Gorms' at one end of the field, the 'Klingons' at the other and the 'Star Ship Enterprise' in the centre. The 'Gorms' and the 'Klingons' try to join forces without being intercepted by the 'Enterprise'. If the 'Enterprise' Cubs catch either a 'Gorm' or a 'Klingon', they are taken to the leader 'Captain Kirk', and his assistant 'Mr. Spock', who will ask them an Arrow Test question. If they answer correctly, they will be allowed back to their end of the field. If they give the wrong answer, then they must remain out until another prisoner is brought to 'Captain Kirk' and 'Mr. Spock' when they will have a chance to answer another question.

Once a 'Gorm' and a 'Klingon' meet they join forces against the 'Enterprise'. If they succeed in capturing a member of the Star Ship crew they take him for the same questioning. A point is awarded for each catch and the winner is the side with the greatest number of points.

Note: Each group should wear a distinguishing mark such as caps on, sleeves rolled up or scarves tied round their arms.

Crocker

Equipment: 2 base posts; 1 large ball; 1 rounders bat.

The Pack divides into two teams and the Captains toss for batting. One post is placed as the wicket and the other stands 4 metres (4 yds.) away to the left of the batsman.

The fielding team spreads out and appoints a bowler who throws the ball to the first batsman. If he hits the ball, or indeed if the ball touches him at all, he must run round the post on his left and back to the wicket before the ball is returned to the bowler. As soon as the bowler has the ball, he bowls again whether the batsman has returned to the wicket or not. This continues until the batsman is caught or clean bowled. A score is kept of the runs made.

Huntsman's Ball

Equipment: 1 tennis ball.

One Cub is the 'Huntsman' and holds the tennis ball which is his 'Spear'. The rest of the Pack are 'Animals' and wear their scarves in their belts. They space themselves out in the field and the 'Huntsman' tries to hit them below the knees with the ball. If he succeeds they put their scarves round their necks and help the 'Huntsman' by throwing the ball back and forth to catch the 'Animals'.

The last 'Animal' left is the winner.

Non-stop Cricket

Equipment: 1 bucket; cricket bat; tennis ball; ball of string; 12 skewers.

Preparation: A circular pitch is marked out using the string and skewers, about 10 metres (10 yds.) in diameter. The bucket, which is the wicket, is placed in the centre.

The Pack divides into two teams and the captains toss for batting. The first man in takes his place before the bucket with the cricket bat and the rest of his team line up near by. The fielding side space themselves out round the pitch, any of these Cubs may bowl from any part of the circumference. The batsman is out if:

    (*a*) The ball hits the bucket.
    (*b*) He is caught off his bat.
    (*c*) He is run out.

One run is to the circumference and back, and one foot must touch the line. When one batsman is out the next team-mate must immediately run in and defend the wicket; there should be no pause in the bowling.

Note: There is no L.B.W. The fastest game on record!

Acknowledgements

In 1969 the Editor of *Scouting* magazine (or *The Scouter* as it was then called) invited members of the Movement to send details of games which they had found successful in their Cub Scout Packs and Scout Troops. The response was overwhelming and material started to arrive from all parts of the United Kingdom.

The process of reading through and categorising the various games was initially undertaken by Joyce Trimby and Nigel Frankland. In some cases the same game was duplicated by various contributors; some of the games were new and others were updated versions of popular favourites.

In making the final selection for publication we are aware that we have had to leave out a number of popular and useful games. These have been kept and will, we hope, form the basis of further collections to be published in the future.

We acknowledge with grateful thanks the many contributions we have received—without them this book could not have been published. Indeed, it would be impossible to publish the names of all those who have contributed. We owe a considerable debt also to the writers of previous games books for many of the ideas published here and adaptations of games which have appeared before. We are told that there are only ten games in the entire world—invented by the Chinese thousands of years ago. So it seems that all our efforts are merely variations on ten themes! If we have poached then we must apologise, but if the games can still provide enjoyment and fun for youngsters in our space age perhaps we may be forgiven.

The companion volume to this—*Scout Games*—is also published by The Scout Association.

Index

Index

Index

Index

* These games do not require any equipment or preparation.

Notes

Notes

Notes

Notes

Notes